THIS IS HISTORY!

The Trenches

THIS IS HISTORY!

The Trenches

A KEY STAGE 3 INVESTIGATION INTO LIFE IN THE TRENCHES
DURING THE FIRST WORLD WAR

DALE
BANHAM

CHRISTOPHER
CULPIN

Hodder Murray

A MEMBER OF THE HODDER HEADLINE GROUP

The Schools History Project

The Project was set up in 1972, with the aim of improving the study of History for students aged 13–16. This involved a reconsideration of the ways in which History contributes to the educational needs of young people. The Project devised new objectives, new criteria for planning and developing courses, and the materials to support them. New examinations, requiring new methods of assessment, also had to be developed. These have continued to be popular. The advent of GCSE in 1987 led to the expansion of Project approaches into other syllabuses.

The Schools History Project has been based at Trinity and All Saints College, Leeds, since 1978, from where it supports teachers through a biennial Bulletin, regular INSET, an annual Conference and a website (www.tasc.ac.uk/shp).

Since the National Curriculum was drawn up in 1991, the Project has continued to expand its publications, bringing its ideas to courses for Key Stage 3 as well as a range of GCSE and A level specifications.

Note: The wording and sentence structure of some written sources have been adapted and simplified to make them accessible to all pupils, while faithfully preserving the sense of the original.

Words printed in SMALL CAPITALS are defined in the Glossary on pages 65–66.

© Dale Banham and Christopher Culpin 2002

First published in 2002
by John Murray (Publishers) Ltd, a division of Hodder Headline Ltd
338 Euston Road
London NW1 3BH

Reprinted 2002, 2003, 2004, 2006

Layouts by Amanda Hawkes
Artwork by Art Construction, Richard Duszczak,
   Oxford Designers and Illustrators, Steve Smith
Typeset in 13/15pt Goudy by Wearset, Boldon, Tyne and Wear
Printed and bound in Dubai

A catalogue entry for this book is available from the British Library

Pupils' Book ISBN–10: 0 7195 8565 1
           ISBN–13: 978 0 7195 8565 4
Teachers' Resource Book ISBN–10: 0 7195 8566 X
           ISBN–13: 978 0 7195 8566 1

◆ Contents

DOES THE FILM THE BATTLE OF THE SOMME PROVIDE A REALISTIC PICTURE OF LIFE IN THE TRENCHES?

Examining the evidence

"Hi! I'm Mr Doc, film producer with Millennium Media. I'm going to be making a film about the First World War. It's going to be BIG and it's going to be TRUE!

You see, Millennium Media knows what the public wants. It wants to know about the lives of the soldiers who fought in the war, but it wants to know the truth. That's what I want: the truth, not the myths. There's a good reason for this: five million people from Britain and the British Empire fought in the First World War. We're talking about your great-grandads. My film will be different because it will show what life was really like for them. Some people have said, 'Why make a film about "ordinary" soldiers?' They're missing the point! The lives these soldiers led in the trenches were truly extraordinary. That's why my film will be IMPORTANT!

I make films that make money. That means a tight schedule and a tight budget. That's where you come in. I need you to help with the research. Your historical skills are just what we need . . . and because of your age you'll be cheap! Are you up for it?

My plan for the film is on the opposite page. I've already thought of a great title – NO MAN'S LAND. Catchy, huh? My two full-time researchers are Mr I. M. Gullible and Ms B. Wary. Fill them in, guys!"

"There's so much source material on this war, we hardly know where to start. But we've already come across one source which could be really useful to Mr Doc. It's a film, made at the time, called *The Battle of the Somme*. It is about one of the most important battles in the war.

This film was seen by over twenty million people.

Because it was made at the time it must be accurate! Mr Doc can use it a lot when he makes his documentary."

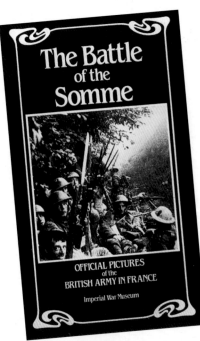

"I'm not so sure. Just because it was made at the time doesn't mean it's accurate."

Mr Doc wants you to write a report for him. He's got four important questions:

- Does the film help to answer the focus questions in his plan (see opposite page)?
- Should we trust *everything* the film tells us?
- Does other evidence support or challenge what the film tells us?
- Overall, does the film provide a realistic picture of life in the trenches on the WESTERN FRONT?

He needs answers and he needs them fast. If you do a good job, Mr Doc might hire you to make a section of the film for him, so do your best!

◆ *The plan!*

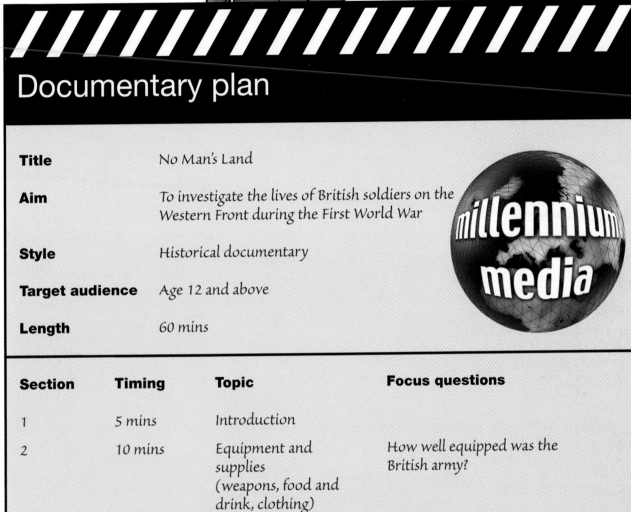

Documentary plan

Title	No Man's Land
Aim	To investigate the lives of British soldiers on the Western Front during the First World War
Style	Historical documentary
Target audience	Age 12 and above
Length	60 mins

millennium media

Section	Timing	Topic	Focus questions
1	5 mins	Introduction	
2	10 mins	Equipment and supplies (weapons, food and drink, clothing)	How well equipped was the British army?
3	10 mins	Trench conditions (sleep, weather, duties, dangers)	How uncomfortable were trench conditions?
4	10 mins	Tactics (British and German tactics, casualty rates)	How effective were the tactics used by the British army?
5	10 mins	Attitudes towards the war	Did soldiers' attitudes remain positive?
6	5 mins	Attitudes towards German soldiers	Was there a real hatred of the the enemy?
7	5 mins	Medical facilities	How well cared for were the wounded?
8	5 mins	Conclusion	

The Battle of the Somme was filmed by Geoffrey Malins and J. B. McDowell. Moving film was still quite new and they were among the first cameramen allowed to film the British army on the battlefields of the Western Front. The film was first shown in London on 10 August 1916. It was put on general release in cinemas across the country on 28 August. At one point, 30 London cinemas were screening the film at the same time.

The Battle of the Somme was a silent film, like all films at the time. Intertitles (captions) were therefore used to explain what the next section of the film was going to show. The film is still available on video so you can see it for yourself.

> ⚠ **WARNING** You need to look at these intertitles very carefully. Film-makers could use them to shape the viewers' response to the moving images that followed.

In a moment you are going to make notes for Mr Doc on what the film tells us about life in the trenches, but before you do read the advice in the panel on the right then practise using the still in Activity A.

> ### ADVICE
>
> **How do I work out what a source is telling me?**
>
> When you examine the film stills or captions, think at two levels:
>
> ■ **Level 1:** What does this source definitely tell me? What obvious information does it give?
> ■ **Level 2:** What does this source suggest? What can I read between the lines? What are the hidden messages?
>
> Level 2 is a lot more difficult! Historians call this important skill making 'INFERENCES' – this means going beyond the obvious facts. The producer of a source often deliberately includes strong hidden messages. These are usually more important than the obvious facts.

ACTIVITY A

Look at the still and intertitle below. Which of the statements in each box **can** be supported by the evidence? Which ones **cannot**? Explain your answer.

What obvious information does the source give me?
- The soldiers were smiling on the evening of the attack.
- German defences had been destroyed.
- Each soldier had a gun, clean uniform and carried a pack.
- Lots of PLATOONS and BATTALIONS from different parts of the country were involved in the battle.
- Medical teams followed the soldiers into battle.

SCENES AT BRAY. PLATOONS OF THE BUFFS, BEDFORDS, SUFFOLKS AND A BATTALION OF THE ROYAL WELSH FUSILIERS MOVING UP ON THE EVENING BEFORE THE ATTACK.

6

What hidden messages does this source convey?
- Soldiers' attitudes towards the war were very positive.
- British tactics were very successful.
- Soldiers were happy to go into battle and were confident of victory.
- The soldiers who fought in the war were part of a large, well-equipped army.
- The quality of medical care for the soldiers was very high.

ACTIVITY B

Now that you have practised on one still, you are going to use the stills and intertitles on pages 8–10 to find out as much as you can about each of Mr Doc's focus questions. The first one has been done for you. You can organise your findings by completing the evidence collection grid below. Keep it safe. You will need it later when you write your report.

We have selected stills and intertitles that we think are most useful but you can use the whole film if you want.

Focus question	Useful stills and intertitles	What do the sources tell us?	What is the key message?
How well equipped was the British army?	8, 9, 15, 17, 18, 25	The British army had a vast supply of shells, very powerful, big guns, destructive bombs and dangerous explosives. The soldiers were well fed.	The British army was very well-fed and equipped. It could easily destroy German defences.
How uncomfortable were trench conditions?			
How effective were the tactics used by the British army?			
Did soldiers' attitudes remain positive?			
Was there a real hatred of the enemy?			
How well cared for were the wounded?			

◆ *Preparations for the battle (25–30 June 1916)*

6

ALONG THE ENTIRE FRONT THE MUNITION 'DUMPS' ARE RECEIVING VAST SUPPLIES OF SHELLS, THANKS TO BRITISH MUNITION WORKERS.   8

HIDDEN BATTERIES WERE POUNDING THE GERMAN TRENCHES FOR FIVE DAYS BEFORE THE ATTACK OF JULY 1ST.

REFILLING LIMBERS WITH 18 POUNDER SHELLS, AFTER 'DUMPING' THE ENEMY CASES.   9

SUPPLY OF 'PLUM PUDDINGS'. THESE BOMBS ARE MOST EFFECTIVE IN SMASHING THE ENEMY'S BARBED WIRE ENTANGLEMENTS. 15

BOMBARDING THE GERMANS WITH 9.2-INCH HOWITZERS. THE SHELLS TEARING UP THE ENEMY'S DEEP DUGOUTS.   17

THE ROYAL WARWICKSHIRES WERE HAVING A MEAL IN CAMP ON THE EVENING BEFORE THE GREAT ADVANCE.   18

OPERATING THE 15-INCH HOWITZER ('GRANDMOTHER') MANNED BY THE ROYAL MARINE ARTILLERY.

FIRING SHELLS WEIGHING 1,400 POUNDS EACH.   25

The Battle of the Somme is available on video from the Imperial War Museum.

◆ *The morning of the attack (1 July 1916)*

JUST BEFORE THE ATTACK.
BLOWING UP ENEMY TRENCHES BY A HUGE MINE. ROYAL ENGINEERS RUSHING OFF TO WIRE THE CRATER FOR OCCUPATION BY THE ADVANCE TROOPS.   29

THE ATTACK. AT A SIGNAL, ALONG THE ENTIRE 16-MILE FRONT, THE BRITISH TROOPS LEAPED OVER THE TRENCH PARAPETS AND ADVANCED TOWARDS THE GERMAN TRENCHES UNDER HEAVY FIRE FROM THE ENEMY.   33

BRITISH TOMMIES RESCUING A COMRADE FROM SHELLFIRE. (THIS MAN DIED 30 MINUTES AFTER REACHING THE TRENCHES.)

CONVEYING THE WOUNDED BY WHEELED STRETCHERS.   34

A LANCASHIRE BATTALION, WHICH HAS BEEN RELIEVED AFTER A SUCCESSFUL ATTACK, RETURNS WITH PRISONERS.
FRIEND AND FOE HELP EACH OTHER.   36

ROYAL FIELD ARTILLERY MOVING UP DURING BATTLE OVER GROUND WHERE THE GORDONS' AND DEVONS' DEAD ARE LYING AFTER A GLORIOUS AND SUCCESSFUL CHARGE ON THE RIDGE NEAR MAMETZ.   37

STRETCHER CASES FOR AMBULANCE.
WOUNDED AWAITING ATTENTION AT MINDEN POST.
SHOWING HOW QUICKLY THE WOUNDED ARE ATTENDED TO.   41

BRITISH WOUNDED AND NERVE-SHATTERED GERMAN PRISONERS ARRIVING.

OFFICER GIVING DRINK, AND TOMMIES OFFERING CIGARETTES, TO GERMAN PRISONERS.   42

THE TOLL OF WAR.
GERMAN DEAD ON THE FIELD OF BATTLE.   49

◆ *After the attack*

1.3 SHOULD WE TRUST EVERYTHING THE FILM TELLS US?

"I knew the film would be really useful. It's no wonder that it has been used so much by TV producers and historians when they need a clip from the First World War. It tells us everything we need to know and covers all the topics in Mr Doc's plan.
      I've also found Source 1 which shows that people at the time thought that it was an accurate account of life in the trenches."

"OK, I admit that the film covers all the topics we need to find out about, but I still think we need to check the accuracy of the film. Good historians don't believe everything a source tells them without carrying out a few checks first!"

SOURCE 1   Review of *The Battle of the Somme* film from *The Times*, 11 August 1916.

In years to come, when historians want to know the conditions . . . they will only have to send for these films and a complete idea of the situation will be revealed before their eyes.

ACTIVITY

As you work through pages 11–16, keep a list of reasons why the film may not be entirely trustworthy.
      Start by looking at the questions asked by each of the source testers in the picture below.

1 Which questions do you think you could answer at this stage?
2 Record any reasons you can think of, at this stage, why the film may not be entirely reliable.
3 Which questions do you think you cannot answer?

SOURCE TESTERS 'R US

CHECK ALL SOURCES VERY CAREFULLY

Check 1: who?
● Who produced it?
● Who were they working for?
● Are they likely to be trustworthy?

Check 2: why?
● Why was the source produced?
● Does it aim to produce a fair and accurate account of the past?
● Is it trying to influence a particular group of people?

Check 3: when?
● When was the source produced?
● How does this affect the potential reliability of the source?

Check 4: what?
● What is included?
● Is it full of fact (something that is known to have happened) or opinion (a point of view)?
● What information does the source fail to give? Why is this?
● Is the source selective in what it includes and what it leaves out?

Decision time
How reliable do you think the film is?
Give it a quality control mark out of five.
1 = totally trustworthy and reliable
2 = very reliable
3 = quite reliable
4 = mainly unreliable
5 = totally unreliable

1. TOTALLY RELIABLE
2. VERY RELIABLE
3. QUITE RELIABLE
4. MAINLY UNRELIABLE
5. TOTALLY UNRELIABLE

◆ *Testing evidence, Part 1: the importance of background knowledge*

To answer all of the questions asked by the source testers, you need to know more about the film's CONTEXT (background). Always consider the PROVENANCE (origins) of a source before you judge its reliability. Think of *why* the source was produced. *The Battle of the Somme* was not produced for the benefit of historians. In order to gain a real insight into the film-makers' intentions you should consider what was happening around the time the source was produced.

ᴀCTIVITY

Use the information on pages 12–14 to complete your own enlarged copy of the graph below to show the success of the ALLIED forces. The plane should rise if the war is going well and drop if it going badly. It will help you place the film in its historical context.

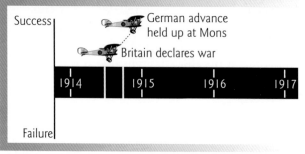

Key events 1914–1916

STAGE 1 August–September 1914

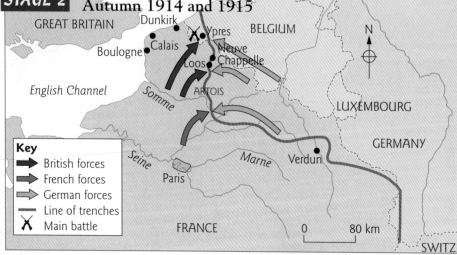

- German troops march into Belgium in August. Britain declares war on Germany.
- German advance across Belgium held up briefly at Mons by the British Expeditionary Force. The British then retreat south to join the French.
- German army marches into France in September. British and French troops halt the German advance at the Battle of the Marne.

STAGE 2 Autumn 1914 and 1915

December 1914
- It is now clear that neither side is going to win a quick victory. Both sides dig a line of trenches stretching from the North Sea to the Swiss border.

March 1915
- British and Indian forces capture the village of Neuve Chapelle.

September–October 1915
- French forces attack the German line in Artois. British forces attack at Loos. Small gains are made but with massive loss of life.

STAGE 3 1916

January
- All able-bodied men are called up for CONSCRIPTION.

February–December
- The Battle of Verdun. German forces attack French forts at Verdun, hoping to wear down the French army. The French know that if Verdun is lost then the road to Paris will be open. They endure a colossal bombardment. Some of the French army refuse to carry on fighting and MUTINY.

The British army has to relieve the pressure on the French. Field Marshal Haig decides on a major attack along the line of the River Somme. He hopes this will force the Germans to move troops away from Verdun and so raise French morale.

READ ALL ABOUT IT

CONSCRIPTION INTRODUCED BY GOVERNMENT

STAGE 4 1 July–19 November 1916, The Battle of the Somme

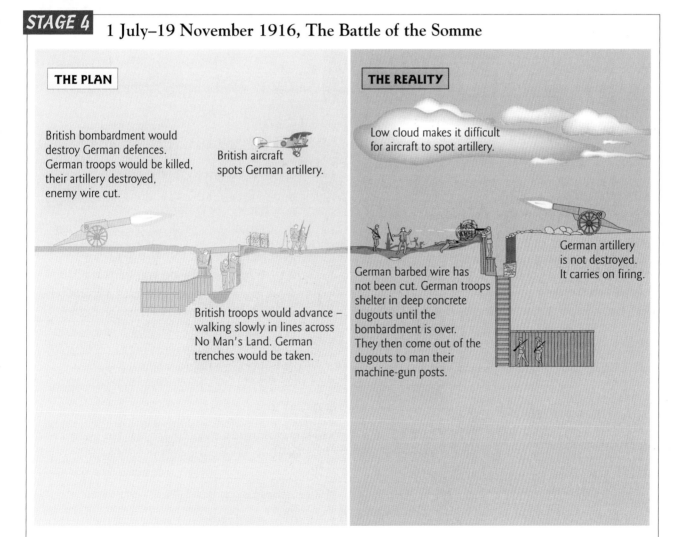

THE PLAN

British bombardment would destroy German defences. German troops would be killed, their artillery destroyed, enemy wire cut.

British aircraft spots German artillery.

British troops would advance – walking slowly in lines across No Man's Land. German trenches would be taken.

THE REALITY

Low cloud makes it difficult for aircraft to spot artillery.

German artillery is not destroyed. It carries on firing.

German barbed wire has not been cut. German troops shelter in deep concrete dugouts until the bombardment is over. They then come out of the dugouts to man their machine-gun posts.

- At the end of June, Allied artillery bombard the German defences.
- The order for the British army to go over the top is given on 1 July. The Allies are confident that nothing will survive the bombardment and that German defences will be destroyed. However, the first day of the battle is a disaster: the worst day in British military history. Casualty figures are over 60,000 (21,000 killed).
- The Battle of the Somme continues until November. By the time Haig calls a halt to the attack, over 400,000 British troops have been killed or wounded. Only 8 km have been gained.

STAGE 5 **August 1916, *The Battle of the Somme* film is released**

- The War Office allows a small group of cameramen to cover the war on the Western Front.
- The cameramen have to depend on the good will of the army units they want to film.
- They are not allowed to record footage without permission.
- The cameramen also do not know how their film will be used. An editing and production team will put the film together for the War Office.
- In August 1916 *The Battle of the Somme* film is released by the British government.
- The government thinks that the film is very important (see Source 2).

SOURCE 2 A letter written by David Lloyd George, Secretary of State for War, which was read to the audience at the first screening of the film.

You are invited here to witness by far the most important picture of the war our staff has yet procured [obtained]. The Battle of the Somme is the most important phase in what is an historic struggle. I am convinced that when you have seen this wonderful picture, every heart will beat in sympathy with its purpose. Every one of us at home and abroad shall see what our men at the front are doing and suffering for us and how their achievements have been made possible by the sacrifices made at home. Now, gentlemen, be up and doing also!

ACTIVITY A

1 Use your graph from page 12 and the background information on pages 12–14 to answer the following questions:
   a) Was the war going well for the British army in 1916?
   b) Why did the British government want to make sure that people at home supported the war effort?
   c) Why was 1916 such a crucial year for:

   ◆ the British army on the Western Front
   ◆ the government's attempt to increase support for the war at home?

2 Read the letter in Source 2 carefully. Why do you think the War Office made the film? Read the following statements. Explain why you agree with, disagree with or need more information before deciding about some of the statements.
   a) The government was making a deliberate effort to cover up the scale of the losses at the start of the Battle of the Somme.
   b) The government aimed to use the film to rally CIVILIAN support for the war effort.
   c) The government was trying to record the Battle of the Somme so that future generations would know what happened.

ACTIVITY B

Look at the source testers' diagram on page 11.

1 Use the background information on pages 12–14 and the extracts from the film on pages 8–10 to put the source *The Battle of the Somme* through each of the quality control checks.
2 Give the film a reliability rating out of five.
3 Explain your rating. Which of the quality control checks did the film fail and which did it pass?

◆ *Testing evidence, Part 2: how is the source written?*

The quality control checks that you have carried out are very important. However, there are two further checks. The way that language is used in a source can give us important clues about the author and how much we should trust what has been written.

LOOKING OUT FOR LOADED LANGUAGE

It is very important to learn how to spot **loaded language**. Newspapers, speeches and even school reports can contain **loaded words** that change the meaning of a whole sentence. The language used can tell us a great deal about the author's views, or what the author is trying to make the reader think. Look at the example below (it is caption 33 from the film). Three words have been fired deliberately into the second sentence. Like bullets, they certainly make an explosive impact!

ADVICE

- The caption includes the detail that the attack took place 'along the entire 16 mile front' in order to demonstrate the size of the British attack.
- The caption claims that British troops **'leaped'** over the parapets. This gives the impression that the British troops were very enthusiastic about the advance.
- The caption claims that the troops advanced 'under heavy fire from the enemy'. This portrays the heroism of the British soldiers, the sacrifices they made and the dangers they faced for their country.

The attack. At a signal, along the entire 16-mile front, the British troops **leaped** over the trench parapets and advanced towards the German trenches under **heavy** fire from the enemy.

ACTIVITY C

1 Look at caption 9 below. Key words or phrases have been highlighted.

> HIDDEN BATTERIES WERE **POUNDING** THE GERMAN TRENCHES **FOR FIVE DAYS** BEFORE THE ATTACK OF JULY 1ST. 9

a) Why are the British batteries **hidden**?
b) What effect does the word **pounding** have?
c) Why do the authors include the detail that the bombardment had been taking place **for five days**?

2 Copy captions 17, 29, 37, 42, 51, 59, 61 (see pages 8–10).

a) Highlight loaded words that have been fired into the sentence.
b) Explain what the producers of the film were hoping to achieve by using these words.

3 Do you now want to change the reliability rating you gave the film? Explain your decision.

ACTIVITY D

This scene was filmed just before the attack. 'Willie' is a nickname for the German Kaiser.

a) Does its caption use loaded language?
b) Rewrite the caption in the same style as the other captions you have looked at. Add some loaded language to get across an important message to your audience. Do not state the obvious!

A soldier poses by a shell with the words 'To Willie With Compliments' on it.

15

◆ *Testing evidence, Part 3: is it authentic?*

A historian also needs to check the AUTHENTICITY of a source – in other words, make sure that it is genuine.

Look again at still 33 on page 9. Is this a genuine shot of men going over the top?

Many historians have argued that the trench does not look very convincing. The footage that follows this shot raises further questions.

ACTIVITY A

Look at the still below.

1 Can you think of any reasons why film-makers might have needed to 'stage' this scene rather than film a real attack?
2 Use Source 3 to check your answer.

SOURCE 3 An extract from the *Viewing Guide to 'The Battle of the Somme' film*, published by the Imperial War Museum in 1987.

In this shot it is hard to see how the cameraman could get his camera into the open so quickly or how he survived there . . . the film clearly includes some material deliberately staged for the camera. This is not to say, however, that the film contains a high proportion of 'faked' material.

ACTIVITY C

1 What reliability rating would you now give the film? Explain your answer.
2 Complete your list of reasons why the film may not be totally trustworthy.

◆ Make sure your list contains a range of reasons based on the work you have completed in this unit.
◆ Keep the list safe. You will need it when you write your report for Mr Doc.

ACTIVITY B

1 Which of the following statements do you agree with at this stage of your investigation? Explain why.
   a) The whole film is unreliable and cannot be used as evidence.
   b) Some of the scenes are unreliable. Other sections of the film need to be checked against other evidence.
   c) The parts of the film that show men going over the top should not be used. The rest of the film is realistic.
2 It is not only films that need to be given the authenticity test. Think of some other sources that also need to be checked.

1.4 DOES OTHER EVIDENCE SUPPORT OR CHALLENGE THE FILM?

"I knew it! You can see why I was so cautious about using the film *The Battle of the Somme* as the main source of information for our documentary. Good documentary film-makers always look at a range of sources before they build their own picture of the past. We can still use the film but clearly it would be unwise to trust *everything* the film tells us. We need to test the key messages contained in the film against other sources. Historians call this cross-referencing. As you can see from the fax below, I have already put together a list of the source material we can use to cross-reference the film."

FAX FROM: 0208 3567 9374
MILLENNIUM MEDIA RESEARCH GROUP   14/01/02 13:31   PAGE 01

millennium media

To: Mr Doc
From: Ms B. Wary
        Millennium Media
        Film Documentary Research Team
RE: Available source material for the documentary *No Man's Land*

There is lots of evidence we can use. No event in history seems to have been so well documented! We have grouped the sources into eight collections:

1. newspapers
2. photographs
3. diaries, memoirs and interviews
4. letters
5. paintings
6. cartoons
7. poems
8. songs.

"Look at the length of this list! We haven't got time to look at all these source collections. Newspapers and photographs will be really useful but surely that will be enough. I mean … why bother with paintings, cartoons or poetry. What can they tell us about life in the trenches?"

DISCUSSION POINT

Do you agree with Mr I. M. Gullible?
a) Do you think that newspapers and photographs will be the most useful source collections?
b) Should paintings, cartoons and poetry be ignored?

◆ *How do I cross-reference effectively?*

"Mr I. M. Gullible is right about one thing – there is lots of source material. It is the rich variety of sources that makes the First World War such a fascinating subject. Many of the sources are really powerful and thought provoking and it is important to examine as many as possible before you reach any conclusions about the accuracy of the film. However, even I could not examine all the sources provided here on my own – you will need to work as part of a research team. Different researchers in your class may look at difference types of source material. Make sure that you share research findings with them. Remember, the more sources you cover, the more convincing your report to Mr Doc will be."

Step 1: establish the key messages that need to be tested.
Before you examine the source collections, you need to be clear about what you are looking for. What key messages from the film do you need to test?

The table below provides some examples of key messages, and shows you how to lay out a **cross-referencing grid**. Fill in one copy of the grid for each source collection.

TABLE A – CROSS-REFERENCING GRID

Topic	Key messages given in the film	Information given in source collection _____	
		How does it support the film?	How does it differ from the film?
Equipment and supplies	• The army was very well equipped. • It had powerful and destructive weapons. • The soldiers had good food and clothing.		
Trench conditions	• The soldiers were clean and well rested. • There were no significant discomforts.		
Tactics	• Preparations before the battle were very effective – German defences were destroyed. • The attack was very successful. • Casualties were low.		
Attitudes towards the war	• The soldiers remained very positive. • They were enthusiastic and fought with great courage.		
Attitudes towards Germans	• There were good relations between British and German soldiers. • German prisoners were very well treated.		
Medical facilities	• Medical facilities were very good. • Wounded soldiers were quickly attended to.		

Step 2: get a feel for the source.
Before you start to examine any source in detail you should consider it as a whole, and read written sources all the way through, to gain a general impression of what is being said.

Step 3: record in Table A the ways the source supports or differs from the film.
Note: You may find that some of the source collections do not provide information on all of the key points you need to test. If so, you will need to record this in an evidence evaluation table (see below).

Step 4: for each source collection, decide how useful the evidence is. Use an **evidence evaluation table** like the one below. Think about whether the sources:
a) contain useful information
b) are reliable.

TABLE B – EVIDENCE EVALUATION TABLE

Source collection:	
The advantages of using this source collection to check the accuracy of the film are . . .	The disadvantages of using this source collection to check the accuracy of the film are . . .

Overall, I feel that this source collection is **really useful/quite useful/not at all useful** for an investigation into life in the trenches.

This is because . . .

◆ Source collection 1: newspapers

How did newspapers report the first day of the Battle of the Somme?

1 Study Sources 1 and 2. What does each report tell you about British tactics?

2 Did contemporary newspapers contain the same messages as *The Battle of the Somme* film? Use a copy of Table A to record similarities and differences.

ADVICE

Using copies of Sources 1 and 2 provided by your teacher, highlight in different colours the sections of the reports which cover the following themes:

- preparations for the attack
- the success of the attack
- British casualties
- German losses.

SOURCE 1 An extract from *The Daily Chronicle*, 3 July 1916.

1st July, 1916: At about 7.30 this morning a vigorous attack was launched by the British army. Before the assault there was a terrific bombardment of the German trenches, which lasted for about an hour and a half. It is too early as yet to give anything but the barest particulars . . . but the British troops have already occupied the German front line. Many prisoners have already fallen into our hands; our casualties have not been heavy.

SOURCE 2 The front page of the *News of the World*, 2 July 1916.

BRITISH ADVANCE

16 MILES OF GERMAN FRONT TRENCHES STORMED

'The Day Goes Well' for our Heroic Troops.

Special Telegrams to the *News of the World*.

British Headquarters, July 1 – Attack launched north of the River Somme this morning at 7.30a.m. in conjunction with French.

British troops have broken into German forward system of defence on front of 16 miles [26 km].

Fighting is continuing.

French attack on our immediate right proceeding equally satisfactorily.

On remainder of British front raiding parties again succeeded in penetrating enemy's defences at many points, inflicting loss on enemy and taking some prisoners.

News to hearten the soul of the nation and inspire it with the highest hopes is contained in the despatch from British Headquarters given above.

Over a front of 16 miles [26 km] north of the Somme the British have stormed the German front line trenches, and Sir Douglas Haig reports that a great battle is raging on the ground to which our gallant troops have penetrated.

On the immediate right of the British the French also attacked with equally satisfactory results.

The depth of the advance varies from one to three miles [1.5–5 km]. Of far more consequence than any mere gain of ground is the work of inflicting upon the enemy heavier losses than those he inflicts upon us. When the enemy has had his fill of punishment he must yield ground.

HOW WE PREPARED. FLOODS OF FIRE FROM OUR GUNS.

Dashing Raids All Along Line.

For a full week we have deluged the German lines with our artillery fire in preparation for the infantry advance. The terrible effect of the British fire has been described from day to day by special correspondents at British Headquarters, whose accounts appear elsewhere. All agree that nothing to equal it has ever occurred before on the British front. Our CURTAIN FIRE had been so effective that the Germans were unable to send food to the front line, with the result that the men in some places had been starving for three days . . .

THE DAY GOES WELL. GALLANT ACHIEVEMENTS OF BRITISH TROOPS.

Capture of Important Points.

British Headquarters, France, July 1, 1.15p.m. – Our troops are making good progress into the enemy territory beyond the front line.

We have taken Serre and Montauban, two important tactical points respectively to south-east of Hébuterne and north-east of Bray.

Our troops are fighting in the villages of Mametz and Contalmaison, parts of which they hold.

Our troops are fighting in a most gallant manner, and many prisoners have been taken in the front lines.

The French are advancing on our right with great steadiness and gallantry, and, after the assault, very quickly covered $1\frac{1}{4}$ miles [2 km] beyond the enemy front line, capturing Curlu and Faviers Wood.

So far the day goes well for England and France.

Can we trust what the newspapers tell us?

ACTIVITY B

1 Look back at the information about the Battle of the Somme on page 13. Using your copies of Sources 1 and 2, highlight in other colours evidence to support the following:

   a) newspapers lied about what was happening during the Battle of the Somme

   b) newspapers reported accurately what was happening during the battle

   c) newspapers often contained vague details about the battle because they could not get specific details.

2 Newspapers used **loaded language** to describe what was happening on the Western Front. Look at Source 2. The attacks made by the troops are called **dashing raids**.

   Make a list of the words used in Source 2 to describe:

   a) the British troops

   b) British gunfire.

3 Try to spot some more examples of loaded language.

4 What impact do you think this kind of language had on people reading the newspaper?

DISCUSSION POINT

> So far as Britain is concerned, the war could not have been fought for one month without its newspapers.

The speech bubble above contains the words of John Buchan who was a leading member of the British government's Department of Information, which produced PROPAGANDA to help the war effort.

Why did Buchan think that newspapers played such a crucial role in the war?

Why was it difficult for newspaper reporters to tell the truth?

SOURCE 3 An extract from *Traveller in News*, a book written by William Beach Thomas about his reporting of the Battle of the Somme for the *Daily Mail* and the *Daily Mirror*.

A great part of the information supplied to us by the British army was utterly wrong and misleading. For myself, on the next day and yet more on the day after that, I was thoroughly and deeply ashamed of what I had written, for the very good reason that it was untrue. Almost all of the official information was wrong.

> I'm a journalist. I should tell it like it is, shouldn't I?

ACTIVITY C

1 Why did William Beach Thomas find it difficult to report the Battle of the Somme accurately?

2 Make a list of any other reasons why it may have been difficult for newspapers to report on events accurately.

3 In groups, play the front page simulation game on pages 22–23. When you have finished, add to your list of reasons why it was difficult for newspapers to report on events accurately.

4 What are the advantages and disadvantages of using newspapers to check the accuracy of the film? Record your ideas on a copy of Table B.

Telling it like it is? The front page simulation game

You are going to produce the front page of a British newspaper in 1917. The date is 3 August and it is three days into the Third Battle of Ypres. Follow the stages below.

Stage 1: events take place

ADVICE

Read page 23. This gives you:

- an outline of the key events that occurred in 1917
- important details about the first three days of the battle.

Stage 2: the army decides what information to pass on to reporters

I agree. We shouldn't tell them too much. Now, what time's dinner?

ADVICE

The government and generals often kept important details about the war from reporters. They feared that crucial information could be given away to the enemy and that negative reports could damage morale.

Imagine that you are a general in the army. Decide what information you would give reporters, then use it to write a summary of the battle.

Stage 3: the reporter writes an article

ADVICE

Reporters who criticised the war effort might be seen as 'traitors' and punished.

- Use your summary from Stage 2 to write a newspaper article on the first three days of the battle. (See Source 2 on page 20 for ideas on how it should look.)
- Your main aims are to:
  — reassure your readers that the war is going well
  — increase support for the war effort back home.
- Use loaded language to achieve your aims. Use the word lists you wrote for Activity B on page 21.

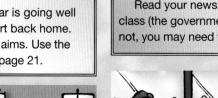

This is all a bit vague, but at least it shows the war is going well.

Stage 4: the newspaper report is edited

ADVICE

Newspaper editors saw it as their duty to support the war effort. As a result, they tended to select information that showed the war was going well. Lloyd George told C. P. Scott of the *Manchester Guardian* in 1917: 'If the people really knew, the war would be stopped tomorrow. But of course they don't – and they can't – know.'

Look carefully at the article you have just written. Edit it carefully.

- Are there any words that you could change to make the message more positive?
- Are there any details that need to be removed from or added to the article?

Careful, my boy. I don't think the public need to know about that.

EDITOR

Stage 5: the final check at the censors

ADVICE

The Defence of the Realm Act was passed on 8 August 1914. This prohibited reports or statements that were likely to undermine loyalty to the King or hinder recruitment. Newspapers were tightly controlled throughout the war. Government CENSORS made sure that articles would not damage morale or the war effort in any way.

Read your newspaper report out to the rest of the class (the government censors). Does it pass the test? If not, you may need to make some last-minute alterations!

We'll have to change that – it will damage morale.

The Third Battle of Ypres: background

◆ The Allies believed that 1917 would be the year in which Germany would be defeated.

◆ Their hopes were raised when, in March, they were able to advance with little resistance into territory held by the Germans. However, hope was short-lived. The Germans knew that British and French forces were about to attack and withdrew to the very strongly fortified Hindenberg line. This made it even harder for the Allies to break through.

◆ A major French attack failed. This was too much for some battle-weary French troops; about 30,000 soldiers deserted.

◆ Haig believed that it was still possible to break through the strongly defended German line near Ypres. The attack was planned for 31 July.

The Third Battle of Ypres

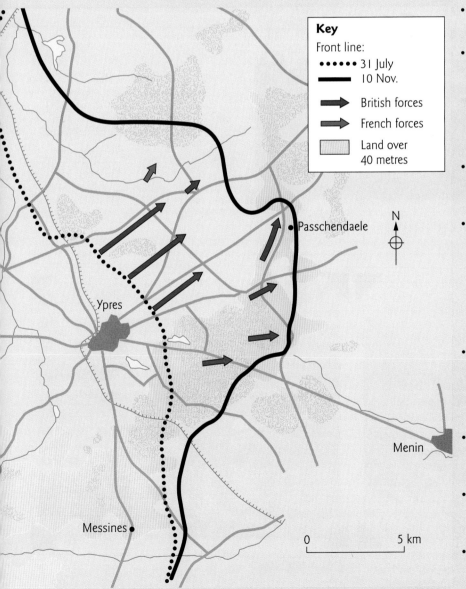

Key

Front line:
- • • • • • 31 July
- ━━━━━ 10 Nov.
- ➡ British forces
- ➡ French forces
- ▨ Land over 40 metres

Passchendaele

N

Ypres

Menin

Messines

0   5 km

- The Allies' aim was to capture the Passchendaele ridge. This would mean an advance of approximately 8 km.
- The Germans were determined to defend the ridge every metre of the way. They were well prepared for the attack. For two years they had been building a line of concrete strong points. These were very well camouflaged and could not be detected by observation planes.
- The situation was made even more difficult by the weather. Constant rain through the summer had turned the area into a quagmire.
- At dawn on 31 July, following a 3000 gun barrage, 100,000 troops went over the top along a 24-km front. The Third Battle of Ypres had begun. At four o'clock in the afternoon it began to rain. Soldiers faced appalling conditions. In many places the water spilled over the top of the shell holes. Men and horses simply vanished in pools of mud.
- In the first two days of the battle, the Allied forces were able to push the Germans back 1.5 km in places. This was further than previous assaults in the area but nowhere near as far as Haig had hoped.
- By the end of the third day, 5000 German prisoners had been captured, but the Allied attack had failed to achieve a breakthrough.
- Despite heavy casualties, attacks on the German front line continued. The Passchendaele ridge was finally captured in November.
- By the time the battle had ended, the British army had suffered nearly 245,000 casualties.

◆ *Source collection 2: photographs*

What can photographs tell us?

"I think that photographs are going to be our most useful source of information. They 'freeze' historical moments and provide an excellent opportunity to find out what life was really like in the trenches. Also, we don't have to worry about all those reliability checks. After all, the camera never lies, does it?"

ACTIVITY

1 Look at the collection of photographs on pages 24–26. Use them to fill in a copy of Table A.

> **ADVICE**
> - Remember that one photograph might tell us about more than one theme.
> - Use the same skills that you developed when you examined the film stills. Always look for the hidden messages!

2 What are the advantages of using these photographs as evidence to check the accuracy of the film? Record your answer on a copy of Table B.

SOURCE 4 Men of the Worcestershire Regiment on their way to the front line, 28 June 1916.

SOURCE 5 British howitzers in action on the Somme, 1916.

SOURCE 6 Two British soldiers with two German prisoners of war, La Boisselle.

SOURCE 7 Stores for the British forces in France and Flanders piled up at Boulogne.

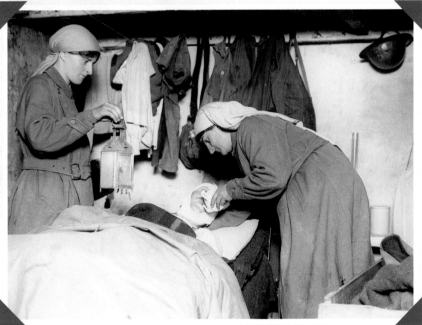

SOURCE 8 Two British nurses tend a wounded soldier.

SOURCE 9 British soldiers blinded by a German gas attack, April 1918.

SOURCE 10 British dead on the battlefield, March 1915.

Who took the photographs?

During the First World War Britain had sixteen official war photographers. Most of them were JUNIOR OFFICERS in the British army. At the start of the war soldiers were allowed to carry their own cameras and sell their pictures to newspapers. This practice was later banned because the government wanted greater control over what photographs were shown to the public.

Many of the photographs taken by official war photographers were not shown during the war because the government thought they might undermine the war effort. Some of the photographs you have just seen were only released after the war.

SOURCE 11 A German corpse on the British wire.

" 'The camera never lies.' What a load of rubbish! You should always think very carefully (something my colleague is not very good at doing) when you use photographs as evidence. Always assume that whoever has published the photograph wants you to believe something. Consider what this 'something' is! During the First World War, the government only allowed 'suitable' photographs to be published. These would often show one or more of the following themes:

◆ the comradeship and high spirits of the soldiers
◆ plentiful supplies of food, clothing and ammunition
◆ German prisoners as tokens of victory
◆ reassuring scenes of impressive British weaponry
◆ slightly injured soldiers being well cared for."

ACTIVITY A

1 Look again at the photographs on pages 24–26. Which do you think the government would not have allowed to be published until after the war? Explain your answer.
2 Read Ms B. Wary's comments on the right. Match each of the photographs that you think were published during the war with one or more of the themes given by Ms B. Wary.
3 Make a list of any other themes the government might want to put across using photographs.
4 You are a picture editor for a British newspaper. Which one photograph from pages 24–26 would you choose to increase support for the war effort in Britain? Explain your choice.

... and why?

A Before

SOURCE 12 CAPTAIN Guy Chapman, 13th Battalion, The Royal Fusiliers.

The whole battalion, except the cooks and the half-dozen officers who had been left out of the attack, was asleep. They lay stretched on the hill side, their faces and hands brown with mud, their hair tangled and their unshaven cheeks bloodless, just as they had fallen in attitudes of exhaustion [Photo A]. There was a sudden stir. A few men rose, others woke and joined them, collecting in a mob round a khaki figure with a camera. German helmets, caps, bayonets and automatics were produced from haversacks. The faces which ten minutes earlier had seemed to be those of dying men were now alight with excited amusement. 'Come on, come an' have your picture took' echoed from man to man; and amid much cheering, the photograph was taken [Photo B].

B After

ACTIVITY B

1 Read Source 12. What disadvantage of using photographs does Chapman highlight?
2 What are the other disadvantages of using photographs to check the accuracy of the film?
3 Complete your copy of Table B for photographs. Have your views on the usefulness of photographs for your enquiry changed? Was Mr Gullible right, does the camera *never* lie? Explain your decision in your conclusion.

◆ *Source collection 3: diaries, memoirs and interviews*

Can we trust what soldiers themselves say?

1: DIARIES

SOURCE 13 An extract from the diary of Captain Maurice Mascall, Royal Garrison Artillery.

15 December 1914

We have been shot into the 'Great War' very suddenly. We arrived yesterday morning. It was rather extraordinary getting into war conditions so soon, but as we advanced we got the whole show brought home to us more and more – the motor-cycle despatch riders tearing about, two aeroplanes over our heads, some fresh graves by the roadside. We were guided to the trenches by an Infantry Officer. It was quite an exciting walk after coming straight from home – bullets singing over our heads, and a more or less continuous fire from snipers on both sides.

The trenches themselves were quite different from anything I had imagined. They have been so often filled with water and rebuilt that nothing much was visible except seas of mud and holes full of water, and filthy but cheerful men standing about the bombproof shelters!

ACTIVITY A

1 Use a copy of Table A to record ways in which Sources 13 and 14 support the film.
2 Why would it be dangerous to use Sources 13 and 14 as evidence that:
   a) soldiers' attitudes remained positive throughout the war
   b) there was no real hatred of German soldiers?

SOURCE 14 SECOND LIEUTENANT Dougan Chater, 2nd Battalion Gordon Highlanders, describing the Christmas Truce, 1914.

Christmas Day

I think I have seen one of the most extraordinary sights today that anyone has ever seen. About 10 o'clock I was peeping over the parapet when I saw a German waving his arms, and presently two of them got out of their trenches and came towards ours. We were just going to fire on them when we saw they had no rifles so one of our men went out to meet them and in about two minutes the ground between the two lines of trenches was swarming with men and officers of both sides, shaking hands and wishing each other a happy Christmas.

For the rest of the day nobody has fired a shot and the men have been wandering about at will on the top of the parapet. We have also had joint burial parties with a service for some dead – some Germans and some ours – who were lying out between the lines. Some of our officers were taking groups of English and German soldiers. This extraordinary truce has been quite unrehearsed, there was no previous arrangement and of course it has been decided that there is not to be any end to our hostilities. We are at any rate having another truce on New Year's Day, as the Germans want to see how the photos come out …

SOURCE 15 An extract from the diary of SERGEANT S. V. Britten, 13th Battalion, The Royal Highlanders of Canada.

22 April 1915

Left at 6.30p.m. for reserve trenches. Just rat holes! One hell of an accommodation! No trenches at all in places, just isolated mounds. Found German's feet sticking up through the ground. The GURKHAS had actually used human bodies instead of sandbags. Beside the stream where we were working, stench something awful and dead all round. Water rats had made a home of the decomposed bodies. Visited the barbed wire with Rae – quit about 1a.m., came back to our dugouts and found them on fire. Found our sack of food had been stolen and we were famished. Certainly a most unlucky day, for I lost my pipe in the evening also. Bed at 4a.m.

23 April

Up about noon and had no breakfast. Furious shelling started about 4.30p.m., and we took to the dug-outs. Almost suffocated by the poisonous fumes. Terrible day, no food or water, dead and dying all around.

24 April

Dug ourselves in on left flank approaching St Julien. Just got finished about 3p.m. At 7.30, trench blown to hell, and we terribly cut up. At 8.10, took message to COLONEL through artillery fire, entered St Julien, and found him transferred to farmhouse outside. Brought him and six others up to the trenches with all the ammunition we could.

ACTIVITY B

1 Read Source 15. Use your copy of Table A to record ways in which this source both supports and challenges the film.
2 Do you think that Source 15 gives you a better insight into soldiers' experiences on the Western Front than Sources 13 and 14? Explain your answer.

ACTIVITY C

1 Read Mr I. M. Gullible and Ms B. Wary's comments below. Record any comments that you agree with in a copy of Table B.
2 Add any other advantages and disadvantages that you can think of.
3 Complete your conclusion.

"Surely we can trust diaries. After all, what is the point in lying to yourself? Diaries are really useful. They tell us a lot about the personal views and attitudes of the soldiers who wrote them. They can also show how individual soldiers were affected by events, and help historians build up a picture of everyday life at a particular time and place."

"I disagree. You have to be careful when you use diaries. They are just a record of one soldier's feelings at a particular point in time. Diaries are often jotted down quickly and only present an event from one point of view. How do we know that one soldier is typical? His thoughts and experiences may be very different from those of the majority of soldiers on the Western Front."

2: MEMOIRS

Memoirs are different from diaries – they are written to be published.

ACTIVITY D

Read Sources 16–20. Use your copy of Table A to record ways in which these memoirs support or challenge the accuracy of the film.

SOURCE 16 An extract from *Diary of a Dead Officer*, the memoirs of A. West, published in 1918.

Brutal injections. The same quantity given to every man regardless of his condition. Dying men made to sit up and smile. Doctors looked on every man as a skrim-shanker [*someone who was pretending to be ill in order to escape the front line*]. Brutal treatment of men unwilling to undergo a particular cure. Men wounded and minus an arm forced to have electric treatment. Knocked down and held on the bed.

Men confined to bed could not relieve themselves without bed pans but no one to bring them. People nearly crying with pain. Gloomy buildings with bathroom taps all loose and tied to the wall with string. Case of a man who came from the front to see his brother. Not allowed in because he had no pass. Meals never hot, worse than ordinary camp food.

SOURCE 17 An extract from *Passchendaele and the Somme*, the memoirs of M. Quigley, published in 1928.

Our division had the task of attacking Passchendaele [in 1917]. None of us knew where to go when the barrage began. A vague memory of following the shellbursts. The whole affair appeared rather good fun. You know how excited one becomes in the midst of danger. I looked at the barrage as something provided for our entertainment. I never enjoyed anything so much in my life – flames, smoke, SOSs, lights, drumming of guns, swishing of bullets.

SOURCE 18 An extract from *Goodbye To All That*, the memoirs of Robert Graves, published in 1929.

From the morning of September 24th to the night of October 3rd, I had eight hours sleep. I kept myself awake and alive by drinking about a bottle of whisky a day. We had no blankets, greycoats, or waterproof sheets, nor any time or material to build new shelters. The rain poured down. Every night we went out to fetch in the dead of other battalions. After the first day or two the corpses swelled and stank. I vomited more than once while supervising the carrying.

SOURCE 19 An extract from *A PRIVATE in the Guards*, the memoirs of Stephen Graham, published in 1919.

A good soldier was one who would not take a prisoner. If called upon to escort prisoners to the cage, it could always be justifiable to kill them on the way and say they tried to escape . . . Captain C., who at Festubert shot two German officer-prisoners with whom he had an argument, was always a hero, and when one man told the story, 'That's the stuff to gi' 'em" said the delighted listeners.

SOURCE 20 Two extracts from *With a Machine-Gun to Cambrai*, the memoirs of George Coppard, published in 1969.

Extract 1

On Christmas Eve we were told not to meet the Germans. For my friends and myself we were in no mood for any joviality with Jerry. Since Loos [1915] we hated his bloody guts. Christmas Day: no parcels, no letters. Soggy rations – plus a few raisins covered in hairs from inside a sandbag. That night we saw some Jerries laying wire. Snowy and I took a machine gun, a hail of bullets and the ghostlike figures fell. Good will to all men meant nothing to us then.

Extract 2

Coppard describes what he saw the morning after the first day of the Battle of the Somme.

We gunners looked at the dreadful scene in front of our trench. Immediately in front, and spreading left and right until hidden from view, was clear evidence that the attack had been brutally repulsed. **Hundreds of dead, many of the 37th Brigade, were strung out like wreckage washed up to a high-water mark. Quite as many died on the enemy wire as on the ground, like fish caught in the net. They hung there in grotesque postures. Some looked as though they were praying; they had died on their knees and the wire had prevented the fall.** It was clear that there were no gaps in the German wire at the time of the attack. It was so dense that daylight could barely be seen through it. How did our planners imagine that Tommies, having survived all the other hazards, would get through the German wire? Any Tommy could have told them that shell fire lifts wire up and drops it down, often in a worse tangle than before.

ACTIVITY A

Re-read the section of Source 20 that is in bold type.

1 Look at the style of writing. How is it different from the style in which diary accounts are written?
2 Why do you think the style of writing differs?

ACTIVITY B

Read Ms B. Wary's comments below. To what extent do you think the points she makes apply to Sources 16–20?

"Memoirs have a number of disadvantages and should be treated with caution.

◆ The author may exaggerate certain events in order to make their memoirs more interesting to the reader and so sell more copies of their books.

◆ The author may exaggerate their own role in events in order to make themselves appear more heroic."

ACTIVITY C

Fill in your copy of Table B. Do you agree with Ms B. Wary? Are memoirs closer to fact or to fiction?

3: INTERVIEWS

"Interviews are a terrifically vivid piece of unofficial history. They allow us to see the war as the soldiers saw it."

DISCUSSION POINT

Do you agree or disagree with Mr I. M. Gullible?

ACTIVITY D

Use Sources 21–23 to fill in your copy of Table A. These three sources are taken from *Voices and Images of the Great War* by Lyn Macdonald. The book was first published in 1988. All three soldiers are describing their experiences during the Battle of the Somme.

SOURCE 21 An interview with CORPORAL H. Diffey, 15th Battalion, Royal Welsh Fusiliers.

We did not go into action until the 10th July 1916. As we approached the village of Mametz there were scores and scores of 18-pounders [guns], wheel to wheel, firing away without any camouflage whatever, and half a mile behind scores of horses waiting to be coupled up to the guns to chase the enemy back to Berlin; but it didn't happen. Months later the guns had hardly moved.

I and a dozen others were told to collect ammunition outside Mametz village. The boxes were very heavy to carry with one's own equipment, but we soldiered on down the road with fountains of earth spouting up each side of the road from enemy shells. Stopping for a rest, I and another chap tumbled into a trench and a second later there was a terrific bang. Returning to the road I came across a scene of complete devastation. There were six bodies and ammunition thrown everywhere as if a giant had smashed the boxes. I was in a daze, a couple of stretcher bearers did what they could for the poor devils.

Then came an order that you must not stop to help a wounded comrade during an attack. Those that did were sitting targets for enemy machine-gunners. Nobody knew what was happening or supposed to happen. And newspapers in the UK wrote of tremendous victories and killing Germans as a sport similar to ratting. We could laugh aloud at these reports, plagued by lice and living amongst the debris of war.

SOURCE 22 An interview with Private W. Hay, 9th Battalion, Royal Welsh Fusiliers.

We were sent into High Wood in broad daylight in the face of heavy machine-gun fire and shell fire, and everywhere there was dead bodies all over the place where previous battalions and regiments had taken part in previous attacks. We were sent in there and C company got a terrible bashing there. It was criminal to send men in broad daylight, into machine-gun fire, without any cover of any sort whatsoever. There was no need for it; they could have hung on and made an attack on the flanks somewhere or other, but we had to carry out our orders.

There was one particular place just before we got to High Wood which was a crossroads, and it was hell there, they shelled it like anything, you couldn't get past it, it was almost impossible. There were men everywhere, heaps of men, not one or two men, but heaps of men everywhere, all dead. Then afterwards, when our battle was all over, after our attack on High Wood, there were other battalions went up and they got the same! They went on and on. They just seemed to be pushing men in to be killed and no reason. There didn't seem to be any reason. They couldn't possibly take the position, not on a frontal attack. Not at High Wood. They couldn't take it against machine guns, just ridiculous. It was absolute slaughter. We always blamed the people up above. We had a saying in the army, 'The higher, the fewer'. They meant the higher the rank, the fewer the brains.

SOURCE 23 An interview with Corporal W. H. Shaw, The Royal Scots 1st/9th Battalion.

Our artillery had been bombing that line for six days and nights, trying to smash the Germans' barbed-wire entanglements, but they hadn't made any impact on those barbed-wire entanglements. The result was we never got anywhere near the Germans. Never got anywhere near them. Our lads was mown down. They were just simply slaughtered. It was just one continuous go forward, come back, go forward, come back, losing men all the time and there we were, wondering when it was going to end. You couldn't do anything. You were either tied down by the shelling or the machine-guns and yet we kept at it, kept on going all along the line, making no impact on the Germans at all. If some of the battalions did manage to break through, it was very rare and it was only small scale.

When the Germans were counter-attacking, well, they were mown down, just the same as we were, and yet they were urged on by their officers just the same as our officers were urging us on. They were coming over just like cattle, whole battalions of them. You just felt, 'You've given it to us, now we're going to give it to you,' and you were taking delight in mowing them down. Our machine-gunners had a whale of a time with those Lewis machine-guns. You just couldn't miss them.

ACTIVITY A

Look at the possible disadvantages of using interviews that Ms B. Wary gives below. What is the main disadvantage of using Sources 21–23 to test the accuracy of the film?

"These interviews should be treated with caution.

◆ The soldiers in Sources 21–23 were all interviewed a number of years after the First World War. Their accounts may be inaccurate if they are forgetful or have a one-sided view of an event.

◆ Interviewees' feelings may have changed over time. They may have been influenced by information or images they saw at a later date.

◆ An interview only represents one person's opinion. We don't know if it is typical of what other soldiers thought and felt.

◆ Interviewers can choose the topics they want interviewees to talk about. Key details can therefore be missed."

ACTIVITY B

Fill in your copy of Table B.

◆ *Source collection 4: letters*

Did soldiers hide 'the truth' when they wrote home?

"Letters are a good source of evidence. They were produced during the war by the soldiers themselves and they give a real insight into soldiers' attitudes. Letters help us understand the soldiers who wrote them: how they were affected by events, why they acted as they did and the conditions in which they lived."

"I'm not so sure. Letters are often very disappointing and unexciting. Most of them deal with minor, day-to-day details and tell us little.

Soldiers wanted to reassure loved ones back home, so they rarely expressed their true feelings.

They also knew that their letters had to pass the censors and that they could be punished if they gave away important military secrets or expressed negative attitudes."

ACTIVITY C

Use Sources 24 and 25 to fill in a copy of Table A.

SOURCE 24 A letter written by Rifleman Bert Bailey of the 11th Battalion, Rifle Brigade. He had married his young wife on 5 June 1915 whilst on leave. He was killed just a few hours after writing this letter.

> *Wednesday, 27 October, 1915*
>
> *My Darling Wife,*
> *Another night has passed and another morning come and I am still in the trenches and in good health. Although all day and night on Monday it rained steadily, yesterday it broke fair and fine and we had a nice day except that underneath everything was mud and slosh. We were employed all morning and afternoon in putting down boards along the trenches and have greatly improved it for walking.*
>
> *Just a few words now about your last parcel. I do appreciate the rag you sent me, it is so very useful. It is grand to wrap my bread in and keep my food clean and nice. Please stop sending tea, sugar and salt for a bit, Darling, as I have plenty. That pastry of your own make was absolutely A1, and a perfect success – and she's the little girl who said, 'Oh, I can only cook a plain dinner'.*
>
> *You must not worry about me, Darling, because I am just as able to look after myself as the other chaps. So dearest little one, just keep cheerful and enjoy yourself all you can, and wrap up now the cold is here. Now love, I will answer the other letters later. I'm afraid I twaddle a lot but never mind.*
>
> *I remain ever your own devoted*
> *Bert.*

DISCUSSION POINTS

1 How useful are these letters in helping you assess the accuracy of the film?

2 Why might Bailey and Stubbs (Sources 24 and 25) be unwilling to express their true feelings about the war and their living conditions?

SOURCE 25 A letter written by Major T. D. H. Stubbs of the Royal Artillery, in 1916.

My dear little Katherine,

Many thanks for your nice letter which I received yesterday. It was good of you to write such a nice letter. We live here more like rabbits than anything else and we have a lookout rabbit who blows three blasts on his whistle when he sees a German aeroplane then we all dive below and remain there until our lookout blows one blast. The German aeroplanes have a horrid habit of coming out just as our dinner and tea is being brought up, the men carrying the meals have to squat down perhaps 100 yards [90 metres] away. We sit in our rabbit holes and peep out at our dinners as the dinners get cold. Three days ago our airmen went up after one of the Germans and shot him down, he also did the same thing with another the day before yesterday so that is two less anyway to bother us.

I am very well indeed and really am liking the life, if only we don't get too many shells at us. We are now getting enough to eat if only the horrid German aeroplanes will leave us alone to eat it. Give my love to Mummy and heaps to yourself. I know you will be good and will make Mummy happy.

Your own
Daddy

ACTIVITY

1 Read Source 26. Use your copy of Table A to record ways in which this letter either supports or challenges the accuracy of the film.
2 In what ways does this letter differ from Sources 24 and 25? Why do you think this is?
3 On a copy of Source 26 provided by your teacher, highlight any section of the letter that would have been cut by army censors.
4 Who do you agree with most – Mr I. M. Gullible or Ms B. Wary? Use your answer to help you fill in a copy of Table B.

SOURCE 26 A letter written by Private Leonard Hart of the 5th New Zealand Reinforcements.

France
19 October, 1917

Dear Mother, Father and Connie,

In a postcard which I sent you about a fortnight ago, I mentioned that we were on the eve of a great event. Well, that great event is over now, and luckily I have once again come through without a scratch.

For the first time in our history as an army, the New Zealanders failed in their objective with the most appalling slaughter I have ever seen. My COMPANY went into action 180 strong and we came out 32 strong. Still, we have nothing to be ashamed of, as our commander afterwards told us that no troops in the world could possibly have taken the position, but this is small comfort when one remembers the hundreds of lives that have been lost and nothing gained.

Our brigade received orders to relieve a brigade of Tommies. At dusk we set off in full fighting order. The weather for some days had been wet and cold and the mud was in places up to the knees. For those five miles [8 km] leading to our front line trench there was nothing but utter desolation, not a blade of grass, or tree, numerous tanks stuck in the mud, and for the rest, just one shell hole touching another. The ground was strewn with the corpses of numerous HUNS and Tommies, yet no attempt had been made to bury any of them. Well, we at length arrived at our destination – the front line – and relieved the worn out Tommies. Many of them seemed too worn out to walk. We were at this point half-way up one slope of the ridge we were to try and take. By daybreak we had dug ourselves in and although wet and covered in mud from head to foot, we felt fit for a feed of bread and bully beef for breakfast.

On the third morning we received orders to attack the ridge at half-past five. At twenty past five, and with a roar that shook the ground, our guns opened up. Through some blunder our artillery opened up about two hundred yards [180 m] short of their target and therefore opened right in the middle of us. It was a truly awful time – our men getting cut to pieces in dozens by our own guns.

Eventually our barrage stopped and we all made a rush for the ridge. Upon reaching almost the top of the ridge we found a long line of practically undamaged German concrete machine-gun placements with barbed wire entanglements in front of them fully fifty yards [45 m] deep! The wire had been cut in a few places by our artillery but only sufficient to allow a few men through at a time. Dozens got hung up in the wire and shot down before their comrades' eyes. It was now broad daylight and what was left of us realised that the day was lost. We lay down in shell holes or any cover we could get and waited. Any man who showed his head was immediately shot. We had lost nearly 80 per cent of our men and gained about three hundred yards [270 m] of ground in the attempt. This three hundred yards was useless to us for the Germans still held and dominated the ridge.

I have just decided to have this letter posted by someone going on leave to England, so I will tell you a few more facts which it would not have been advisable to mention otherwise. Some terrible blunder has been made. Someone is responsible for the barbed wire not having been broken up by our artillery. Someone is responsible for the opening up of our barrage in the middle of us instead of 150 yards [140 m] ahead of us. Someone else is responsible for those machine-gun emplacements being left practically intact, but the papers will report another glorious success, and no one except those who actually took part in it will know any different.

During the night before our attack on the ridge we were surprised to hear agonised cries of 'Stretcher-bearer', 'Help', 'For God's sake come here', etc., coming from all sides of us. When daylight came some of us crawled out to the shell-holes from where the cries were coming and were amazed to find about half a dozen Tommies, badly wounded, some insane, others almost dead with starvation and exposure, lying stuck in the mud and too weak to move. One man said if we cared to crawl about in the shell-holes all round about him we would find dozens more. These chaps, wounded in the defence of their country, had been cruelly left to die the most awful of deaths in the half-frozen mud while tens of thousands of able-bodied men were camped within five miles [8 km] of them behind the lines. All these Tommies had been wounded during their unsuccessful attack on the ridge which we afterwards tried to take, and at the time when we came upon them they must have been lying where they fell in mud and rain for four days and nights.

I have seen some pretty rotten sights during the two and a half years of active service, but I must say that this fairly sickened me. We crawled back to our trenches and inside of an hour all our stretcher-bearers were working like the heroes that they were, and in full view of the enemy whom, to his credit, did not fire on them. They worked all day carrying out those Tommies. The fact remains that nothing was done until our chaps came up, and whoever is responsible for the unnecessary sacrifice of those lives deserves to be shot more than any Hun ever did.

We are expecting to move about twenty miles [32 km] back from here tomorrow where we can get fresh reinforcements and thoroughly reorganise. I shall not be sorry to get on the move.

With best wishes,

I remain,
Your affectionate son,
Len

◆ *Source collection 5: paintings*

"During the First World War, the British government's Department of Information commissioned artists to produce paintings for propaganda purposes. The first British war artists were appointed in 1916 and attached to active units in the British army. However, as you will see, some artists were horrified by what they saw. Despite their official positions, they produced paintings that were very critical of the war ... It is often said that a picture paints a thousand words. If we use these paintings carefully they can tell us just as much about the trenches as written sources."

(Ms B. Wary, History of WWI)

ADVICE

How do you unlock a painting's messages?

Using paintings to find out about the past is not easy. You need to apply the same skills you used to investigate the film stills and photographs.

■ Remember to start with the question, 'What does this painting tell me?' Do not rush this stage. You can miss important details if you only take a quick glance.
■ To be as thorough as possible, pretend you are describing the painting on the telephone to a friend who has never seen the picture before. Write down all the details that you need to give for your friend to have a clear idea of what the painting looks like.
■ You then need to make inferences. Try to work out what is being suggested by the artist. Is there an underlying message in the painting?

SOURCE 27 *Over the Top* by John Nash. Nash served in the British army in France from November 1916 to January 1918. The painting is based on an attack that he took part in, in 1917, near Cambrai. The soldiers had to climb out of their own trench, charge towards the enemy trench and try to capture it. Of 80 men in Nash's unit, 68 were killed in the first five minutes of the attack.

ACTIVITY

1 Look at Source 27. Which inference cannot be made from this painting? What is the artist's key message?
2 Use Sources 27–29 to fill in a copy of Table A.
3 Fill in a copy of Table B. Do you agree with Ms B. Wary? Are paintings just as useful as written sources?

Clues: what does this source tell us?
• Sometimes the battlefields were covered in snow.
• Soldiers wore dark brown overcoats.
• The soldiers walked across No Man's Land.
• Some soldiers died when they went over the top.
• The only soldiers left in the trench have been killed or wounded.

Messages: what does this source suggest or infer?
• Soldiers were sometimes dangerously visible to the enemy when they went over the top.
• The Germans had better tactics.
• Casualty rates were very high when attacks took place.
• Tactics were poorly thought out.
• The soldiers on the front line were always close to death.

SOURCE 28 *The Harvest of Battle*, painted in 1919 by
C. R. W. Nevinson. Nevinson joined the Belgian Red Cross in 1914,
and worked as a driver and stretcher-bearer in France. He later became
an official war artist.

SOURCE 29 *Gassed* by John Singer Sargent, an official war artist.
Sargent was sent to France in 1918. This painting was based on scenes
that he saw at a clearing station for victims of a mustard gas attack. It
was painted in 1919.

◆ *Source collection 6: cartoons*

"All the cartoons on pages 38–39 appeared in *The Bystander*, a popular weekly magazine read by soldiers and civilians throughout the war. The cartoons were produced by Captain Bruce Bairnsfather of the Royal Warwickshire Regiment. Bairnsfather served on the Western Front from 1914 and was wounded during the Second Battle of Ypres in 1915. The cartoons reflect his experiences of the war. Bairnsfather himself said, 'I could not draw a trench joke, unless I had lived in the trenches myself.' At first I thought that cartoons would not be useful for our investigation ... but now I'm not so sure. What do you think?"

ADVICE

Unlocking cartoons

Cartoons are not photographs, taken in a fraction of a second. They are created with time and thought. They usually include factual details, and nearly always express the cartoonist's point of view.

Step 1: look at the picture

You need to use all the clues available. You could label all the people and objects in the cartoon (as we have begun to do in Source 1). Then ask yourself the key questions:

■ What do these clues tell us about life in the trenches?
■ Why has the cartoonist included these details in his/her picture?
■ What is the cartoonist's attitude to these details?

Step 2: examine the caption

Does it help you to understand the cartoonist's message?

ACTIVITY A

1 Finish labelling a copy of the cartoon in Source 30 provided by your teacher.
2 What is the main message behind the cartoon?

ACTIVITY B

1 Use Sources 30–34 to fill in a copy of Table A. The cartoons are all by Captain Bruce Bairnsfather.

2 In pairs, discuss the advantages and disadvantages of using this source collection to cross-reference the film. Record your ideas on a copy of Table B.

SOURCE 30

This suggests that it was very noisy in the trenches.

?

?
?
?
?

Getting the Local Colour
In that rare and elusive period known as "Leave" it is necessary to reconstruct the "Atmosphere" of the front as far as possible in order to produce the weekly "Fragment."

SOURCE 31

" ——— these ——— rations."

SOURCE 33

THE INNOCENT ABROAD.

Out Since Mons: "Well, what sort of a night 'ave ye 'ad?"
Novice (but persistent optimist): "Oh, alright. 'Ad to get out and rest a bit now and again."

SOURCE 32

Trouble With One of the Souvenirs

"'Old these a minute while I takes that blinkin' smile off 'is dial"

SOURCE 34

A Matter of Moment

"What was that, Bill?"
"Trench mortar"
"Ours or theirs?"

◆ *Source collection 7: poems*

"Often, when people think of the First World War, they think of the poetry of Wilfred Owen and Siegfried Sassoon. Both of these men fought in the war, but how do we know that their experiences are typical of other soldiers? We need to think twice about using poetry for historical investigations. Poems have their place . . . in ENGLISH lessons! I mean, poets such as Owen and Sassoon are hardly typical soldiers, are they?"

"Ms B. Wary makes an important point about using historical sources. It is dangerous to make **generalisations** about **all** soldiers based on the experiences of just two individuals. However, as I have learnt, it is also unwise to write off a whole source collection without even looking at it! I think Wary's gone too far this time … but you make up your own mind about poetry's usefulness as a source."

ACTIVITY A

1 Poetry can create very powerful images. Imagining the scene can be a good way of getting into a poem.

As you read the first eight lines of 'Dulce et Decorum Est' (Source 35), try to picture what Owen describes. Quickly sketch these images.

2 How do the images of conditions in the trenches differ from the pictures presented in *The Battle of the Somme* film?

3 Read the rest of the poem. Use a copy of Table A to record all the ways in which the images differ from the film.

SOURCE 35 'Dulce et Decorum Est' by Wilfred Owen.

Bent double, like old beggars under sacks,
Knock-kneed, coughing like hags, we cursed through sludge,
Till on the haunting flares we turned our backs
And towards our distant rest began to trudge.
Men marched asleep. Many had lost their boots
But limped on, blood-shod. All went lame; all blind;
Drunk with fatigue; deaf even to the hoots
Of gas-shells dropping softly behind.

Gas! Gas! Quick, boys! – An ecstasy of fumbling,
Fitting the clumsy helmets just in time;
But someone still was yelling out and stumbling
And floundering like a man in fire or lime.
Dim, through the misty panes and thick green light,
As under a green sea, I saw him drowning.

In all my dreams before my helpless sight,
He plunges at me, guttering, choking, drowning.

If in some smothering dreams, you too could pace
Behind the wagon that we flung him in,
And watch the white eyes writhing in his face,
His hanging face, like a devil's sick of sin;
If you could hear, at every jolt, the blood
Come gargling from the froth-corrupted lungs,
Obscene as cancer, bitter as the cud
Of vile, incurable sores on innocent tongues,
My friend, you would not tell with such high zest
To children ardent for some desperate glory,
The old Lie: Dulce et decorum est
Pro patria mori.
[It is sweet and proper to die for one's country.]

INFORMATION

The poetry of Wilfred Owen

Owen served in the front-line trenches of France from January to June 1917, when he was sent back to England suffering from shell-shock. He returned to the front in August 1918, and was awarded the Military Cross in October for exceptional bravery on the battlefield. Owen was killed on 4 November. The news of his death reached his parents on the day that the war ended.

SOURCE 36 'Suicide in the Trenches' by Siegfried Sassoon.

I knew a simple soldier boy
Who grinned at life in empty joy,
Slept soundly through the lonesome dark,
And whistled early with the lark.

In winter trenches, cowed and glum,
With CRUMPS and lice and lack of rum,
He put a bullet through his brain.
No one spoke of him again.

You smug-faced crowds with kindling eye
Who cheer when soldier lads march by,
Sneak home and pray you'll never know
The hell where youth and laughter go.

SOURCE 37 'The General' by Siegfried Sassoon.

'Good-morning; good-morning!' the General said
When we met him last week on the way to the line.
Now the soldiers he smiled at are most of 'em dead,
And we're cursing his staff for incompetent swine.
'He's a cheery old card,' grunted Harry to Jack
As they slogged up to Arras with rifle and pack.

But he did for them both by his plan of attack.

SOURCE 38 An extract from 'Aftermath' by Siegfried Sassoon.

Do you remember the dark months you held the sector at Mametz –
The nights you watched and wired and dug and piled on sandbags on parapets?
Do you remember the rats; and the stench
Of corpses rotting in the front of the front-line trench –
And dawn coming, dirty-white, and chill with a hopeless rain?
Do you ever stop and ask, 'Is it all going to happen again?'

Do you remember that hour of din before the attack –
And the anger, the blind compassion that seized and shook you then
As you peered at the doomed and haggard faces of your men?
Do you remember the stretcher-cases lurching back
With dying eyes and lolling heads – those ashen-grey
Masks of the lads who once were keen and kind and gay?

Have you forgotten yet? . . .
Look up, and swear by the green of the spring that you'll never forget.

DISCUSSION POINTS

1 Read the background information on Sassoon above. Why would it be dangerous to **just** use his poetry to cross-reference the film?
2 What are the advantages of using Sassoon's poetry for your enquiry?

ACTIVITY B

Use your copy of Table A to record ways in which Sassoon's poetry (Sources 36–38) gives different messages from those in *The Battle of the Somme* film.

ACTIVITY A

Use Sources 39–41 to fill in your copy of Table A.

ACTIVITY B

1 Which of the poets in Sources 39–41 displays the most positive attitude towards war?
2 Suggest a possible reason for this.

SOURCE 39 An extract from 'The Soldier' by Rupert Brooke.

If I should die, think only this of me:
That there's some corner of a foreign field
That is for ever England. There shall be
In that rich earth a richer dust concealed;
A dust whom England bore, shaped, made aware,
Gave, once, her flowers to love, her ways to roam,
A body of England's breathing English air,
Washed by the rivers, blest by suns of home.

INFORMATION

The poetry of Rupert Brooke

Brooke was made a sub-lieutenant in the Royal Naval Division and saw some action at Antwerp in 1914, which he described as a 'queer picnic'. He died of blood poisoning in April 1915 on the way to Gallipoli, without ever being engaged in battle.

INFORMATION

The poetry of Richard Aldington

Aldington was born in 1892 and was university educated. He served on the Western Front from 1916 to 1918 where he was badly gassed, the after-effects of which never left him.

SOURCE 40 'Bombardment' by Richard Aldington.

Four days the earth was rent and torn
By bursting steel,
The houses fell about us;
Three nights we dared not sleep,
Sweating, and listening for the imminent crash
Which meant our death.

The fourth night every man,
Nerve-tortured, racked to exhaustion,
Slept, muttering and twitching,
While the shells crashed overhead.

The fifth day there came a hush;
We left our holes
And looked above the wreckage of the earth
To where the white clouds moved in silent lines
Across the untroubled blue.

SOURCE 41 An untitled poem by Sidney Chaplin. Chaplin served in the 4th Battalion of the Gloucestershire Regiment.

You stand in a trench of vile stinking mud
And the bitter cold wind freezes your blood
Then the guns open up and flames light the sky
And, as you watch, rats go scuttling by.

The men in the dugouts are quiet for a time
Trying to sleep midst the stench and the slime
The moon is just showing from over the hill
And the dead on the wire hang silent and still.

A sniper's bullet wings close to your head
As you wistfully think of a comfortable bed
But now a dirty blanket has to suffice
And more often than not it is crawling with lice.

Haig and his mob keep well in the Rear,
Living in luxury, safe in old St Omer,
Flashing Red Tabs, Brass and Ribbons Galore,
What the Hell do they know about fighting a War?

ACTIVITY C

Fill in a copy of Table B. Do you agree with Ms B. Wary that poems are not a good source of evidence for finding out about life in the trenches?

◆ *Source collection 8: songs*

Soldiers in the trenches or behind the lines spent a lot of time singing. In the British army, soldiers wrote songs to fit familiar tunes or they sang old favourites.

SOURCE 42 In Flanders, this song was sung to the tune of 'My Little Grey Home in the West'.

I've a little wet home in a trench,
Where the rainstorms continually drench,
There's a dead cow close by
With her feet towards the sky
And she gives off a terrible stench.

Underneath, in the place of a floor,
There's a mass of wet mud and some straw,
But with the shells dropping there,
There's no place to compare
With my little wet home in the trench.

SOURCE 43 A stanza from 'The Old Barbed Wire'.

If you want to find the old battalion,
I know where they are,
I know where they are.
If you want to find a battalion,
I know where they are,
They're hanging on the old barbed wire.
I've seen 'em, I've seen 'em,
Hanging on the old barbed wire,
I've seen 'em,
Hanging on the old barbed wire.

SOURCE 44 This song was sung by British soldiers in late June 1916, as they moved into position for the Battle of the Somme.

We beat them on the Marne,
We beat them on the Aisne,
We gave them hell
At Neuve Chapelle
And here we are again!

ACTIVITY D

1 Do Sources 42 and 44 tell us more about:
   a) trench conditions (Source 42) and the success of British tactics (Source 44) **or**
   b) the attitudes of British soldiers on the Western Front?
2 Do you think songs like these would have been encouraged by commanding officers?
3 How does the tone of Source 43 differ from Sources 42 and 44?
4 Could Source 43 be used as evidence that soldiers' attitudes were not as positive as Sources 42 and 44 suggest?

ACTIVITY E

1 Use Sources 42–44 to fill in a copy of Table A.
2 Fill in a copy of Table B.

"Wow! I never really knew there were so many different ways of finding out about the past. I've learnt some important lessons about handling historical sources and I won't be jumping to conclusions in the future!"

"Well, I'm glad you've learnt something at last! Critical thinking is important – you must not believe *everything* you are told in life, and it's no good writing off a source collection before you look at it. Even I was caught out by that poetry collection! Anyway, that's the research finished, now for the difficult part – pulling all the evidence together and writing the report for Mr Doc. It's sure to be a bit of a rollercoaster ride …"

ACTIVITY

It is now time to answer the key question: 'Does the film *The Battle of the Somme* provide us with a realistic picture of what it was like to be a British soldier in the trenches?'

Your task is to write a report for Mr Doc that analyses the value of the film for an enquiry into life in the trenches on the Western Front.

This is your chance to organise and communicate your ideas about the film. It is your big chance to impress Mr Doc. Don't blow it! To help you organise your report, go for a ride on the history roller-coaster! It has seven stages. Remember that you already have notes for stages 3, 4 and 5. Stage 5 is quite tricky. You will need to decide how many times you dare loop the loop! Use the advice on pages 46–47 to help you negotiate this stage.

Stage 2: THE INTRODUCTION CLIMB
- Provide a brief background to the film.
- State your aim.

History roller-coaster
ENTRANCE

Stage 1: THE PRE-RIDE CHECK
WARNING! Do not go on this ride if:
a) You are not clear about the question.
b) You are not sure of your argument.
c) You do not have enough evidence to support your argument.

Stage 7: THE EDITING STRAIGHT
Nearly finished ... but don't jump off too soon!
- Have you checked your spelling and punctuation?
- Is each paragraph well structured?
- Are your arguments clear and supported by evidence?

THIS WAY

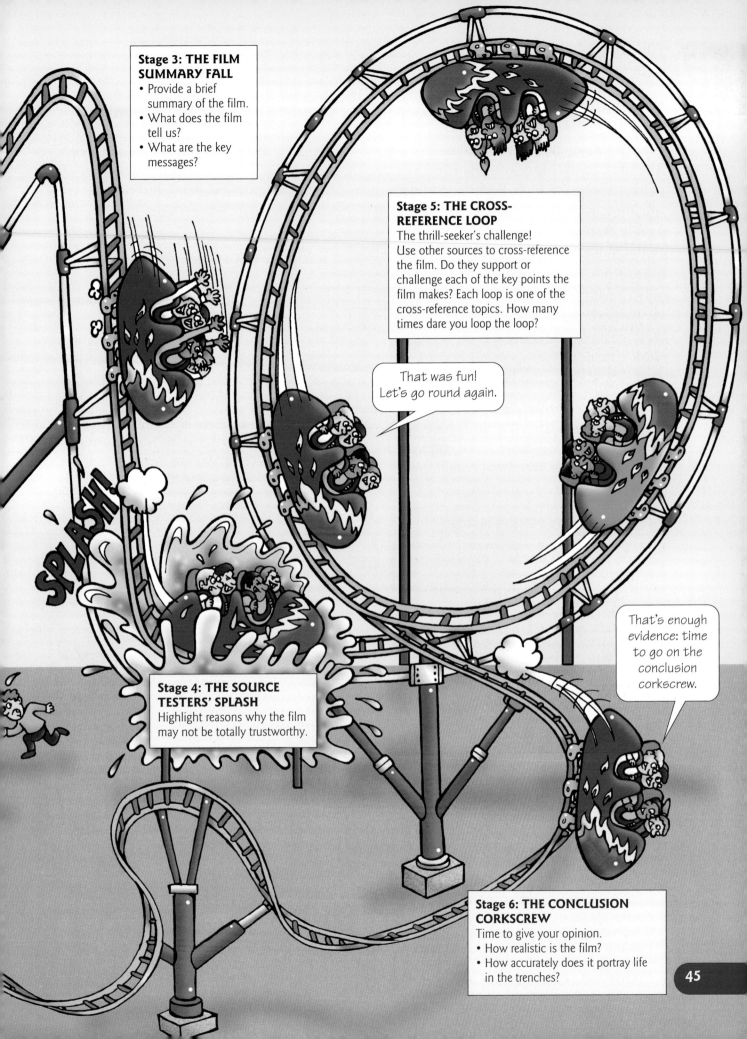

Stage 3: THE FILM SUMMARY FALL
• Provide a brief summary of the film.
• What does the film tell us?
• What are the key messages?

Stage 5: THE CROSS-REFERENCE LOOP
The thrill-seeker's challenge!
Use other sources to cross-reference the film. Do they support or challenge each of the key points the film makes? Each loop is one of the cross-reference topics. How many times dare you loop the loop?

That was fun! Let's go round again.

That's enough evidence: time to go on the conclusion corkscrew.

SPLASH!

Stage 4: THE SOURCE TESTERS' SPLASH
Highlight reasons why the film may not be totally trustworthy.

Stage 6: THE CONCLUSION CORKSCREW
Time to give your opinion.
• How realistic is the film?
• How accurately does it portray life in the trenches?

Tackling the cross-reference loop – how to write a balanced account

Step 1: decide how many loops

You need to decide how many times you are going to loop the loop. Each loop looks at one topic from the cross-referencing grid (Table A, page 18). You should aim to go round at least four times, otherwise your conclusion will lack authority. You must examine how accurately the film portrays:

◆ 1 – Equipment and supplies
◆ 2 – Trench conditions
◆ 3 – Tactics
◆ 4 – Soldiers' attitudes towards the war.

The other two topics (Attitudes towards the Germans and Medical facilities) are optional, but, remember, the more times you loop the loop the stronger your final conclusion becomes!

Step 2: write a paragraph for each loop

Each of the topics you examine will need a carefully planned paragraph. Your aim is to produce a balanced account.

◆ If you have found evidence that both supports and challenges the accuracy of the film, weigh the evidence and reach a balanced conclusion. Structure your paragraph like the model below.
◆ If you have found no evidence to support the film, you need to say so before you go on to look at the evidence that challenges the film.

> ⚠ **WARNING** Do not fall into the trap of using evidence that you have found to be very untrustworthy to support or challenge the film.

Paragraph structure for looping the loop

> The way that the film portrays . . . can be supported by **many/some** of the sources.

- Signpost each new paragraph.
- Use the first sentence to ORIENTATE the reader.
- Outline which aspect of the film you are going to test against other sources.

> The sources suggest that . . .
> For example, . . .
> Some sources also imply that . . .
> This is shown in . . .

- Outline ways in which the film can be supported by other sources.
- Make sure you provide specific examples to support each point using your versions of Table A.
- Try to draw your examples from a range of sources.

> However, other sources challenge the images put forward in the film.
> **Many/some** sources suggest that . . .
> For example, . . .
> In addition, **many/some** sources imply that . . .
> This can be seen in . . .

- Outline ways in which other sources challenge the impression put forward in the film.
- Make sure you provide specific examples to support each point using your versions of Table A.

> Overall, I feel that the evidence **clearly indicates/suggests** . . . that the film provides **a realistic/quite a realistic/quite an unrealistic/ an unrealistic** picture of . . .
> This is because . . .

- Weigh the evidence and make a judgement.
- If you don't find the evidence that supports the film convincing, explain why, using your versions of Table B. It might be because of a lack of evidence or you may feel a particular source or type of source that supports the film cannot really be trusted.

Step 3: check the language in your paragraphs

Think very carefully about the words you use in your concluding statements for each paragraph. If there is a lack of convincing evidence to support a firm conclusion, say so.

Think of the evidence as a bridge that has to support your conclusion. If you have a flimsy evidence bridge, you should not try to drive a juggernaut of a conclusion such as 'The film is totally unrealistic' over it. The evidence will not bear it. The bridge will collapse!

Unless you have a really strong bridge, you need to reach cautious Mini-size conclusions. Use **tentative language** such as 'The film is **quite** realistic' or 'The evidence **suggests** that . . .'

SO YOU THINK YOU COULD DO BETTER?

Drawing your own conclusions

"Thanks for your report. Very interesting! Clearly life in the trenches was far worse than *The Battle of the Somme* film makes out. But one thing really puzzles me. If conditions were so terrible, why on earth did British soldiers carry on fighting?

Over and over again they charged against barbed wire, facing almost certain death. Yet no one seems to have questioned orders.

Read Source 1. Can you explain why men like Lieutenant Wallace and Private Russell carried on fighting? If you can, perhaps we should include a section about this in the documentary.

Historians have suggested many reasons why men continued to fight. My researchers have narrowed it down to six main reasons, but we can't make up our minds which is the most important. Can you?"

ACTIVITY

1 Read explanation 1. Why do you think lists of executed soldiers were read out at army parades?
2 Read explanation 2. Why do you think soldiers were given rum before they went over the top?

SOURCE 1 Private Henry Russell's account of going over the top during the Battle of the Somme.

During our advance, I saw many of my colleagues killed by German machine-gun fire, but this somehow or other did not seem to worry me and I continued to go forward until I suddenly became aware that there were few of us left capable of going on.

I found myself in the company of an officer, Lieutenant Wallace. We dived into a flat, shallow hole made by our guns, not knowing what to do next ... I came to the conclusion that going on would be suicidal and that the best thing we could do would be to stay there and pick off any Germans who may expose themselves. Lieutenant Wallace said, however, that we had been ordered to go on at all costs and that we must comply with this order. At this, he stood up and within a few seconds dropped down riddled with bullets. This left me with the same problem and having observed his action, I felt I must do the same. I stood up and was immediately hit by two bullets and dropped down.

Explanation 1: The 'sticks' of army discipline

Men continued to fight because they were afraid of being punished if they did not.

◆ 1540 soldiers who refused to fight in the war were condemned to two years' FORCED LABOUR. Of these, 71 died as a result of their ill-treatment.
◆ Soldiers could be executed for desertion, cowardice, mutiny and a range of other offences. Lists of those executed were read out at parades.
◆ A common punishment was Field Punishment Number 1, or 'crucifixion' as the soldiers called it. The man was tied to a fixed object for up to two hours a day and for up to three months.

Explanation 2: The 'carrots' of reward

Soldiers continued to fight because of the 'rewards' they gained for doing so.

◆ Soldiers were awarded medals for military service, and could be promoted far more quickly than in civilian life.
◆ Many accounts of army life emphasise the importance of decent accommodation and warm clothing.
◆ Morale was also very dependent on good rations (food and drink). For some soldiers, their daily diet in the army was better than at home. There are reports of soldiers gaining 2.5 cm in height and 6 kg in weight within a month of joining the army.
◆ Alcohol and cigarettes also helped. Men were given rum before they went over the top.
◆ Entertainment was provided to help maintain morale. Soldiers were entertained by professional and amateur concerts, saw films at field cinemas and played football.

Explanation 3: The habit of obedience

Soldiers continued to fight because the society they lived in taught them a sense of duty.

◆ Many soldiers came from jobs in which they were used to following orders.
◆ British society in the early twentieth century taught people to respect those of 'higher rank'.
◆ Education was very strict. Children were taught to obey commands and were punished if they stepped out of line. People were not expected to question what they read or interpret things for themselves.

You must learn to do as you're told, boy! Now learn these dates off by heart before the end of the lesson.

Explanation 4: Patriotism

◆ Schools stressed to children the importance of loyalty to their country, love for their nation and the willingness to defend their family. This meant that men stood by their country as they would a lifelong friend.
◆ To die fighting for your country and saving others was seen as glorious, as this extract from a popular school reading book shows:

To die young, clean . . . to die swiftly, in perfect health; to die saving others from death, or worse disgrace; . . . to die and to carry with you into the better life beyond the grave, hopes and ambitions, unembittered memories, all the freshness and gladness of May – is that not a cause for joy rather than sorrow? (An extract from *The Hill* by H. A. Vachell, published in 1905.)

For King and country!

DISCUSSION POINTS

1 How has education and society changed since the early twentieth century?
2 Does this mean that you would react differently if placed in the same situation as the soldiers who fought in the First World War?

Explanation 5: Comradeship – the bonds that existed between soldiers

Men continued to fight because they did not want to let their friends down.

◆ Firm friendships were built between men who fought alongside each other. There was a real sense of 'being in it together'. Soldiers shared the same experiences and helped each other ease the fear and insecurity of life in the trenches.
◆ Peer pressure made it difficult to appear different from other men. A coward would be mocked.
◆ A shared sense of humour made the suffering bearable. British soldiers gave comic names to the things around them. A cemetery became a 'rest camp'; going over the top became 'jumping the bags'. Many soldiers were able to laugh not only at themselves and at others, but at the horrors of war itself.

I'm really scared, but I'm not going to show it. I don't want to let my mates down.

Explanation 6: The joy of war

Soldiers carried on fighting because they enjoyed it.

◆ For some soldiers the sense of danger made the war very exciting.
◆ Some soldiers enjoyed the challenge – they saw war as the ultimate test.

This is so exciting! It beats the boring job I used to do – at last, I've really got a chance to prove myself.

◆ *Winning debates – the seven steps to success*

HOW TO WIN DEBATES

ACTIVITY

Your task is to use pages 50–55 to prepare for a debate: 'What was the main reason why men stayed in the trenches and carried on fighting'.

"Great speeches have made history but if you want to win the debate you'll need more than a good speech. Follow the seven steps to success very closely and remember everything you have learned about using each form of evidence."

Step 1: use a sorting frame to organise the available evidence

Explanation	Sources that support	Sources that challenge	Rating	Reason
I STICKS Army discipline				

Copy this table to compare the explanations given on pages 50–51. Fill out columns 2 and 3 using Sources 2–13 on pages 52–55. You may need to think more carefully about some sources. Look at Source 2, for example. How can it be used to support two of the explanations. What are they?

Step 2: use your sorting frame to make a decision
After studying the sources you should have some evidence to support each explanation. Which explanation is supported by the most convincing evidence? Give each explanation a rating out of five. The higher the score, the more convincing the evidence is. Explain each rating.

Time to make a decision. This is not the time to sit on the fence!

SOURCE 2 A cartoon by Captain Bruce Bairnsfather.

Bruce Bairnsfather

"**The Spirit of our Troops is Excellent**"

Step 3: write an effective speech

◆ Use the available evidence to write a persuasive speech that supports your decision.

◆ Aim to explain your ideas clearly and concisely.

◆ Support your arguments by referring to specific sources. You can use sources from this unit (pages 52–55) or from Unit 1.4 (pages 20–43).

◆ You will have a set time limit in which to deliver your speech. Stick to it, and use the time effectively.

◆ Remember what you have learnt from previous study units about how to structure an effective speech. It should look something like the double hamburger below.

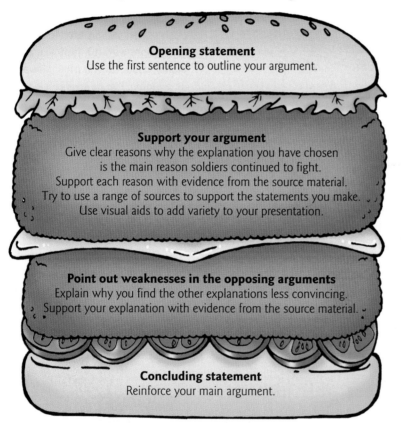

Opening statement
Use the first sentence to outline your argument.

Support your argument
Give clear reasons why the explanation you have chosen is the main reason soldiers continued to fight.
Support each reason with evidence from the source material.
Try to use a range of sources to support the statements you make.
Use visual aids to add variety to your presentation.

Point out weaknesses in the opposing arguments
Explain why you find the other explanations less convincing.
Support your explanation with evidence from the source material.

Concluding statement
Reinforce your main argument.

Step 4: think about how to deliver your speech

◆ Proofread your speech. Make sure you can read it and know how to pronounce key words.

◆ Test the quality of your speech by reading it to a partner. Listen to any criticism and make improvements.

◆ Add emphasis to key points, for example by repetition.

◆ Vary the length of sentences within a paragraph to give pace, variety and to emphasise key points.

◆ Use persuasive words and phrases throughout your speech such as 'The evidence **clearly demonstrates** that . . .' rather than 'I think that . . .' or 'The evidence **suggests** that . . .'.

Step 5: prepare for the debate

◆ Be prepared to justify and defend your point of view. Try to anticipate the opposition's questions and criticisms. How are you going to defend yourself? Use examples which are linked to your main argument.

◆ Write down questions to use to challenge the opposition. Think of them as the chips or fries to go with your burger!

How can you argue …
when Source …
provides clear evidence that …?

Step 6: during the debate

◆ Listen to the arguments put forward by the opposition. Jot down questions and points with which you disagree.

◆ Answer and ask questions politely. Draw on relevant evidence to support your arguments.

Step 7: after the debate

Review your performance. Note down its high points as well as ways it could be improved. If you lost, learn from your mistakes and make sure you win next time.

Diaries, memoirs and interviews

SOURCE 3 An interview with Trooper Sydney Chaplin of the Northamptonshire Yeomanry.

We were called to Attention and the APM began to read: 'Private So-and-So, you have been charged and found guilty of desertion in the face of the enemy. The verdict of the court martial is that you are to be shot at dawn.' It was signed by Sir Douglas Haig. Next morning the sun was shining and a touch of frost in the air. I was sent up to the road to stop any traffic and being high up and on horseback I had a bird's-eye view. I saw the man brought out to the post and the firing squad march into position, turn right and take up stand. I heard the report as they fired and saw the smoke from their rifles. Then they turned and marched off. The officer, with the revolver in his hand, inspected the body, then turned away. The dead man was then taken away in a blanket and buried in the small cemetery in the next field. It was over. I came down, but it did not seem real.

SOURCE 4 An extract from *Passchendaele and the Somme*, the memoirs of M. Quigley, published in 1928. The author is writing about the events of 1917.

Our division had the task of attacking Passchendaele. None of us knew where to go when the barrage began, whether half left or half right. A vague memory of following the shellbursts as long as the smoke was black, and halting when it came to white came to me. The whole affair appeared rather good fun. You know how excited one becomes in the midst of danger. I looked at the barrage as something provided for our entertainment. I never enjoyed anything so much in my life – flames, smoke, SOSs, lights, drumming of guns, swishing of bullets all appeared stage props to set off a majestic scene.

Letters

SOURCE 7 An extract from a letter by Private J. Bowles, 2nd/16th Battalion, Queen's Westminster Rifles, written in 1916.

The 'rest' we had all looked forward to consists of fatigues, parades of all kinds, and guards. Last Saturday I was sent to Maroeuil on guard, and I am writing this in the sentry box. We expect to be relieved tonight but I don't care if we are not because this isn't a bad 'stunt' and I must say I have enjoyed myself immensely. I was off duty at 6p.m. We cooked our own grub and lived like lords. Eggs and bacon for breakfast, Welsh Rarebit and tea for supper, tinned fruit and cream for tea.

SOURCE 8 An extract from a letter home written by Private Mudd.

Out here dear we're all pals. We share each other's troubles and get each other out of danger. You wouldn't believe the kindness between men out here. It's a lovely thing is friendship out here.

SOURCE 5 An extract from the diary of Captain Julian Grenfell, 1st Royal Dragoons, October 1914.

Four of us were talking and laughing in the road when a dozen bullets came with a whistle. We all dived for the nearest door, which happened to be a lav, and fell over each other, yelling with laughter . . . I adore war. It's just like a big picnic, without the objectlessness of a picnic. I've never been so well or so happy.

SOURCE 6 A quote from Robert Graves, who served in France with the Royal Welsh Fusiliers.

The funny thing was that you went home on leave for 6 weeks or 6 days but the idea of staying at home was awful because you were with people who didn't understand what this [war] was all about.

SOURCE 9 An extract from a letter written by Laurie Rowlands, 15th Battalion, Durham Light Infantry. This letter was written in February 1918.

Not a single man has an ounce of what we call patriotism left in him. No one cares a rap whether Germany has Alsace, Belgium or France too for that matter. All that every man desires now is to get done with it and go home . . . I may add that I too have lost pretty nearly all the patriotism I had left, it's just the thought of you all over there, you who love and trust me to do my share of the job that is necessary for your safety and freedom. It's just that that keeps me going and enables me to 'stick it'.

Photographs and cartoons

SOURCE 10 A cartoon by Captain Bruce Bairnsfather.

The New Submarine Danger
" They'll be torpedoin' us if we stick 'ere much longer, Bill"

SOURCE 11 An official photograph. The caption reads 'Bringing in the wounded. This man is actually under heavy fire. He brought in twenty wounded in this manner.'

Poems

SOURCE 12 'The Deserter' by Winifred Letts. During the war Letts served as a Voluntary Aid Detachment nurse.

There was a man, – don't mind his name,
Whom Fear had dogged by night and day.
He could not face the German guns
And so he turned and ran away.
Just that – he turned and ran away,
But who can judge him, you or I?
God makes a man of flesh and blood
Who yearns to live and not to die.
And this man when he feared to die
Was scared as any frightened child,
His knees were shaking under him,
His breath came fast, his eyes were wild.
I've seen a hare with eyes as wild,
With throbbing heart and sobbing breath.
But oh! It shames one's soul to see
A man in abject fear of death.

But fear had gripped him, so had death;
His number had gone that day,
They might not heed his frightened eyes,
They shot him when the dawn was grey.
Blindfolded, when the dawn was grey,
He stood there in a place apart,
The shots rang out and down he fell,
An English bullet in his heart.
An English bullet in his heart!
But here's the irony of life, –
His mother thinks he fought and fell
A hero, foremost in the strife.
So she goes proudly; to the strife
Her best, her hero son she gave.
O well for her she does not know
He lies in a deserter's grave.

SOURCE 13 'Two Fusiliers' by Robert Graves.

And have we done with War at last?
Well, we've been lucky devils both,
And there's no need of pledge or oath
To bind our lovely friendship fast,
By firmer stuff
Close bound enough.

By wire and wood and stake we're bound,
By Fricourt and Festubert,
By whipping rain, by the sun's glare,
By all the misery and the loud sound,
By the Spring day,
By the Picard clay.

Show me the two so closely bound
As we, by the wet bond of blood,
By the friendship blossoming from mud,
By Death; we faced him, we found
Beauty in Death,
In dead men, breath.

DISCUSSION POINTS

1 Do you think that a section of Mr Doc's documentary should explore why men carried on fighting? If so, for how long should the programme look at this issue?
2 Which part of the documentary would you cut the length of to make way for this new section?

HOW IS THE FIRST WORLD WAR PRESENTED TODAY?

"The accounts that you looked at in Unit 1.4 (pages 17–43) were all produced at the time of the conflict or are the experiences of soldiers involved in the conflict, recorded at a later date. But how is the war presented today? Extracts from two of the most influential recent representations of the war are contained in Sources 1 and 2. Novels and TV programmes have had a significant influence on how people today view the First World War."

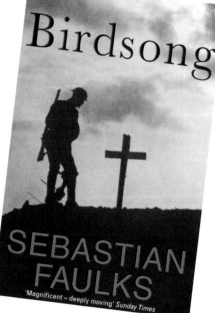

Birdsong

SEBASTIAN FAULKS

'Magnificent – deeply moving' *Sunday Times*

ACTIVITY

Read Sources 1 and 2. What does each source tell us about the following themes:
a) conditions in the trenches
b) the attitudes of the soldiers before an attack
c) the effect of British tactics?

SOURCE 1 An extract from *Birdsong*, a novel by Sebastian Faulks. It was first published in 1993. Faulks did not fight in the First World War.

In this extract, he describes the experiences of a group of soldiers during the first day of the Battle of the Somme.

Eight hours before the revised time of attack the guns went quiet, preserving shells for the morning.

It was night-time, but no man slept . . .

Towards four, the lowest time of the night, there was a mortal quiet along the line. No one spoke. There was for once no sound of birds.

There was at last a little light over the raised ground and mist down by the river. It began to rain.

Gray, urgent, sour-breathed at the head of the communication trench. 'The attack will be at seven-thirty.'

The platoon commanders were stricken, disbelieving. 'In daylight? In daylight?' The men's faces cowed and haunted when they were told.

Breakfast came with tea in petrol cans. Hunt's earnest features bent over bacon on a tiny stove . . .

Then came the rum, and talk began again. Men drank greedily. Some of the younger boys staggered and laughed . . .

The noise overhead began to intensify. Seven-fifteen. They were almost there. Stephen on his knees, some men taking photographs from their pockets, kissing the faces of their wives and children. Hunt telling foul jokes. Petrossian clasping a silver cross.

The bombardment reached its peak. The air overhead was packed solid with noise that did not move. It was as though waves were piling up in the air but would not break. It was like no sound on earth . . .

The mine went up on the ridge, a great leaping core of compacted soil … Flames rose to more than a hundred feet [30 m]. It was too big, Stephen thought. The scale appalled him. Shock waves from the explosion ran through the trench.

Brennan was pitched forward off the firestep and broke his leg.

We must go now, thought Stephen. No word came. Byrne looked questioningly at him. Stephen shook his head. Still ten minutes.

German fire began at once. The lip of the British trench leapt and spat soil where machine guns raked it. Stephen ducked. Men shouting.

'Not yet.' Stephen screaming. The air above the trench now solid.

The second hand of his watch in slow motion. Twenty-nine past. The whistle in his mouth. His foot on the ladder. He swallowed hard and blew.

He clambered out and looked around him. It was for a moment completely quiet . . .

Then . . . the German machine guns resumed. To his left Stephen saw men trying to emerge from the trench but being smashed by bullets before they could stand. The gaps in the wire became jammed with bodies. Behind him the men were coming up. He saw Gray run along the top of the trench, shouting encouragement.

He walked hesitatingly forward, his skin tensed for the feeling of metal tearing flesh . . .

Byrne was walking beside him at the slow pace required by their orders. Stephen glanced to his right. He could see a long, wavering line of khaki, primitive dolls progressing in tense deliberate steps, going down with a silent flap of arms, replaced, falling, continuing as though walking into a gale . . .

He saw Hunt fall to his right. Studd bent to help him and Stephen saw his head opening up bright red under machine gun bullets as his helmet fell away . . .

Stephen went down. Some force had blown him. He was in a dip in the ground with a bleeding man, shivering . . .

The man with him was screaming inaudibly. Stephen wrapped his dressing round the man's leg, then looked at himself. There was no wound. He crawled to the rim of the shellhole. There were others ahead of him. He stood up and began to walk again.

Perhaps with them he would be safer. He felt nothing as he crossed the pitted land on which humps of khaki lay every few yards. The load on his back was heavy. He looked behind and saw a second line walking into the barrage in No Man's Land. They were hurled up like waves breaking backwards into the sea. Bodies were starting to pile up and clog the progress.

There was a man beside him missing part of his face, but walking in the same dreamlike state, his rifle pressing forward. His nose dangled and Stephen could see his teeth through the missing cheek. The noise was unlike anything he had heard before. It lay against his skin, shaking his bones. Remembering his order not to stop for those behind him, he pressed slowly on, and as the smoke lifted in front of him he saw the German wire.

It had not been cut. Men were running up and down it in turmoil, looking for a way through. They were caught in the coils where they brought down torrents of machine gun fire. Their bodies jerked up and down, twisting and jumping. Still they tried. Two men were clipping vainly with their cutters among the corpses, their movement bringing the sharp disdainful fire of a sniper. They lay still . . .

He looked back towards the British line, each foot of which was pathetically exposed to fire from this superior position. Through the smoke of the German barrage he could see the scruffy line still straggling on, driven by some slow, clockwork purpose into the murder of the guns . . .

Stephen presumed that most of the men who had begun the attack with him were dead. The second wave had not reached this far and perhaps never would. He reasoned that he should try to retire and join a later attack, but his orders were to press on past Beaumont Hamel as far as Beaucourt, on the river. The soldier's motto, Price had told the men: when in doubt go forward.

SOURCE 2 Two extracts from 'Goodbyeee', the last programme in the *Blackadder Goes Forth* TV comedy series, first shown in 1989.

EXTRACT 1 SCENE ONE

It is night, it is pouring with rain and the shelling is constant. Blackadder and George have just inspected the troops in the trench. They are ankle deep in mud.

GEORGE   Oh, dash and blast all this hanging about, sir. I'm as bored as a pacifist's pistol. When are we going to see some action?

BLACKADDER   Well, George, I strongly suspect your long wait for certain death is nearly at an end. Surely you must have noticed something in the air?

GEORGE   Well yes, of course, but I thought that was Private Baldrick.

BLACKADDER   Unless I'm much mistaken, soon we will at last be making the final big push, the one we've been so looking forward to all these years.

GEORGE   Hurrah with highly polished brass knobs on. About time!

[The field phone rings: it is on Baldrick's back. Blackadder picks it up.]

BLACKADDER   Hello, Somme Public Baths. No running, shouting or piddling in the shallow end. Oh, it's you, Darling. Tomorrow at dawn. Oh, excellent. See you later then. Bye!

[He hangs up.]

BLACKADDER   Gentlemen – our long wait is nearly at an end. Tomorrow morning, General 'Insanity' Melchett invites you to a mass slaughter. We're going over the top.

GEORGE   Huzzah and hurrah! God Save the King, Rule Britannia and boo sucks to Harry Hun!

BLACKADDER   Or to put it more precisely, you're going over the top, I'm going to get out of it.

[Blackadder and George move to the dugout.]

GEORGE   Oh, come on, Cap! May be a bit risky – but it's sure as bloomin' 'ell worth it, guv'nor.

[Blackadder undresses while George dresses for battle.]

BLACKADDER   How can it possibly be worth it? We've been sitting here since Christmas 1914, during which time millions of men have died, and we've moved no further than an asthmatic ant with heavy shopping.

GEORGE   No, but this time I'm pos. we'll break through – it's ice-cream in Berlin in fifteen days.

BLACKADDER   Or ice-cold in No Man's Land in fifteen seconds . . .

EXTRACT 2 SCENE 4

The next day. Blackadder's attempts to get out of going over the top have failed. Outside is heard the muffled faraway cry: 'Stand to, stand to, fix bayonets!'

BLACKADDER   Come on, come on, let's move.

[They all move out. At the door, Blackadder turns to George.]

Don't forget your stick, Lieutenant.

GEORGE   *[picking up his stick]* Rather, sir. Wouldn't want to face a machine-gun without this.

[They emerge in the misty trenches and all stand in line, ready for the off. Then suddenly there is a silence.]

DARLING   I say, listen – our guns have stopped.

GEORGE   You don't think . . .

BALDRICK   Perhaps the war's over. Perhaps it's peace.

GEORGE   Hurrah! The big nobs have got round the table and yanked the iron out of the fire.

DARLING   Thank God – we lived through it – The Great War, 1914 to 1917.

ALL THREE   Hip hip hurray!!!

BLACKADDER   I'm afraid not. The guns have stopped because we are about to attack. Not even our generals are mad enough to shell their own men. They feel it's more sporting to let the Germans do it.

GEORGE   So, we are, in fact, going over. This is, as they say, it?

BLACKADDER   Yes, unless I can think of something very quickly.

[A command is heard: 'Company, one pace forward.' They all take one pace forward.]

BALDRICK   There's a nasty splinter on that ladder, sir. A bloke could hurt himself on that.

[A call: 'Stand ready.' They put their hands on the ladders, ready to climb over.]

I have a plan, sir.

BLACKADDER   Really, Baldrick, a cunning and subtle one?

BALDRICK   Yes, sir.

BLACKADDER   As cunning as a fox who's just been appointed Professor of Cunning at Oxford University?

BALDRICK   Yes, sir.

[Another call is heard: 'On the signal, Company will advance.']

BLACKADDER   Well, I'm afraid it's too late. Whatever it was, I'm sure it was better than my plan to get out of this by pretending to be mad. I mean, who would have noticed another mad man round here?

[A whistle goes. He looks at Baldrick.]

Good luck everyone.

[Blackadder blows his whistle. There is a roar of voices – everyone leaps up the ladders. As they rise above the sandbags they are met by thunderous machine-gun fire. Blackadder, Baldrick, George and Darling run on . . . They will not get far.

Silence falls. Our soldiers fade away. No Man's Land turns slowly into a peaceful field of poppies. The only sound is that of a bird, singing sweetly.]

"Novels such as *Birdsong* and TV programmes such as *Blackadder* tell us more about what it was really like in the trenches than *The Battle of the Somme* film."

ACTIVITY

1   Study how 'Goodbyeee' ends. Why have the writers ended the programme in this way? What is their key message to the audience?

2   What do Sources I and 2 tell us about the way that we look at the First World War today?

3   Compare Sources I and 2 to *The Battle of the Somme* film. Why is the impression of life in the trenches so different?

4   To what extent do you agree with Mr I. M. Gullible's statement?

"So, I guess by now you think you're an expert on the First World War? Well, you could be just the person I'm looking for. I need someone with vision, intelligence and imagination – someone a bit like myself – who could make a film from all this! All the sections of *No Man's Land* have been carefully planned, except the last five minutes – the conclusion. This is by far the most difficult part of the film to plan.

In the conclusion we need to pull together all the different threads from the other sections of the programme and make our final statement to the audience. Do you think you can help?

You'll need to use a storyboard like the one opposite to plan the final scenes of the documentary. The conclusion should have between six and ten scenes. Remember, these are the most important scenes of the whole programme. They need to be interesting and informative. I hope you're up to the challenge. I'm looking forward to seeing what you come up with."

Clearly, what Mr Doc needs is a good historian – someone who is imaginative, thoughtful and rigorous in the way he or she presents the past. What Mr Doc has asked you to do will test a very important skill: **your ability to reconstruct the past**. You need to show that you can link together evidence from different sources to produce a convincing and reasoned account of the past. The sources you use should be powerful but also ones that the audience can trust.

Piecing together what it was like to be a soldier on the Western Front is difficult. Different sources contain different messages and some sources were produced for propaganda purposes, or were heavily censored. Good historians are not put off by these difficulties. They think critically about the sources they use but do not give up when they encounter sources that are selective or untrustworthy. They consider all the angles and try to produce the most accurate account possible.

ACTIVITY A

Look at the trouble-shooting table below.
Working in pairs:
a) add any other problems you can think of
b) think of a possible solution to each problem.

Problem	Possible solution
It is often difficult to reach firm conclusions.	Use tentative language. For example, say 'The evidence **suggests** ...' rather than 'The evidence **shows** ...'; say '**Many** soldiers ...' rather than '**All** soldiers ...'
Some sources were produced for propaganda purposes or may have been censored.	

ACTIVITY B

Work in pairs to plan your conclusion to *No Man's Land* using the storyboard structure on page 61. Use any of the sources in this book to support statements you make or as visual aids.

Scene number	Words	Visual image	Type of shot	Sound effect
6	Conditions in the trenches were terrible. Men faced many dangers and discomforts. Gas attacks were particularly feared, as the following extract from a poem by Wilfred Owen shows ...	The painting *Gassed* by John Singer Sargent (see page 37).	Full shot of painting then the camera zooms in on the face of one of the soldiers lying in the foreground.	The eerie hissing sound of gas escaping then men screaming.

Scene Number
Number each scene. Do not have too many (aim for between six and ten). Remember that you have only five minutes for the conclusion to the documentary.

Words
Indicate which words are going to be spoken by the presenter. If you are using a source such as an extract from a poem or part of a letter, it is a good idea to use a different reader. Keep your writing clear and concise.

Visual image
Support what you are saying with visual images. Aim to include one per scene. You can use sources contained in this book, such as photographs and cartoons, or you can sketch or take your own pictures. For example, as a closing image you could include a picture of your local war memorial or, like the makers of *Blackadder*, you may want to end with a popular image such as a field of poppies.

Type of shot
Indicate what movements you want the camera to make. If, for example, you are using a painting, do you want the camera to show the whole painting, then zoom in on a particular section? You should also indicate whether you are using black-and-white or colour pictures.

Sound effects
Try to think of appropriate sound effects to accompany each scene. The sound of wind and heavy rain could accompany a photograph of a soaked soldier in a muddy trench. Alternatively, you may think that a particular piece of music captures the mood of a scene. You could play it softly in the background as the presenter speaks or use it to accompany visual images.

DISCUSSION POINTS

Look at the scene on the storyboard above.

1 What photograph from pages 24–26 could you use instead of the painting?
2 Look again at the poem 'Dulce et Decorum Est' (page 40). Which lines would you use for Scene 6?

◆ *Designing your own First World War website*

One of the most important skills you have learnt from your study of the First World War is how to handle evidence. This includes:

- gaining information from a source (by **making inferences** and spotting the hidden clues as well as the obvious ones)
- **thinking critically** about what you have been told (after all, it is dangerous to believe everything you see or read)
- testing what you have been told by using a range of other sources (**cross-referencing**)
- using evidence carefully to form your **own opinions** about the past.

Now it's time to pass on your knowledge to students of the future!

ACTIVITY

In groups, construct your own website about the First World War. The purpose of your site is to provide advice for future Year 9 pupils studying life in the trenches on how they should handle the available source material.

- **Your website should cover all the source types you used in Unit 1.4.** What were the advantages and disadvantages of using each source collection? Which source collections would you recommend? Which source collections need to be treated with caution?
- **The site could also contain advice on using *Birdsong* and *Blackadder* (Unit 2.2).** How useful are they as evidence?
- **You will not need to do any extra research.** Use the copies of Tables A and B that you completed during Unit 1.4 and reflect on your work in Units 2.1 and 2.3. Which sources helped you to establish the reasons why men carried on fighting? Which sources helped you reconstruct the past and design your conclusion to Mr Doc's film?

ADVICE

When constructing your website, remember the following.

- Your target audience is Year 9 pupils. Make sure that your website is attractive and accessible to them.
- Design an opening page to introduce the site, then allow one web page for each source type.
- Lay out each web page in a similar style to the one opposite.
- Make sure that you cover both the advantages and disadvantages of using each type of source. Provide at least one example to support each statement.

millennium media

Internet Browser

Back　Forward　Stop　Refresh　Home　AutoFill　Print　Mail

Address: @ |　　　　　　　　　　　　　　　　　　　　　　　　　　〉go

| SOURCE COLLECTION TITLE | ICON |

Advantages
There are a number of advantages in using ... to investigate life in the trenches.

Firstly, ...
For example, sources such as ... [click here to see the source]

... are also useful because ...
... is a good example of this [click here to see the source]. It ...

Finally, ... help us ...
For example, Source ... describes how ... [click here to see the source]

Disadvantages
However, ... do need to be treated with caution. This is because ...
An example of this can be seen in Source ... This source ...

Another potential problem is that ...
This is illustrated in Source ... which ...

Finally, ...

Conclusion
Overall, ... are very useful/ quite useful/ of limited value for
investigating what life was really like for soldiers on the Western Front.
This is mainly because ...

| ADVICE |

If you conclude that a particular source type is only of
limited value for an investigation into life in the trenches,
indicate what this source type would be useful for. For
example, you might conclude your web page on using
newspapers by saying:
'Newspapers would be more useful for an enquiry into
propaganda techniques used by the British government.
This is because ...'

◆ *Skills appraisal*

ACTIVITY A

Look at the computer screen below.
a) Which new skills have you learnt through studying this book?
b) Which skills have you improved?
c) Which skills do you need to develop further?
d) Which skills would also prove useful in other subjects?
e) Which skills will be useful to you in later life?

ACTIVITY B

Look at the statements that have been highlighted on the computer screen. Are these the three most important things that you have learnt through studying the First World War?

Write an e-mail to the student in the picture explaining whether you agree or disagree with the choices he or she has made.

What have you learnt from studying the First World War?

How to handle evidence
I have learnt ...
• how to use a wide range of sources
• how evidence can be manipulated by governments and the media
• how propaganda and censorship can affect how events are reported
• how to cross-reference the messages contained in a source
• how to analyse texts critically
• how to reconstruct the past from conflicting sources.

How to organise and communicate my own ideas and arguments
I have learnt how to ...
• write clear, well-organised reports
• produce a balanced essay
• write in a persuasive style
• deliver powerful speeches
• prepare for and take part in debates
• design film scripts and websites
• write for a range of different audiences.

How ordinary men lived extraordinary lives during the First World War
I have learnt ...
• what life was really like for the soldiers who fought on the Western Front
• why millions of men continued to fight despite the dangers and discomforts
• that the human story of those who fought in the war is just as important as studying the causes, key events and the results of the First World War.

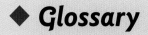 Glossary

ALLIES the group of countries that agreed to support each other in the event of an attack from Germany

ARTILLERY a section of the army that uses large guns

AUTHENTICITY a measure of something being genuine and trustworthy

BATTALION a military group made up of three or more **companies**

BATTERY a set of large guns

BOOTY valuable items stolen from the enemy by an army at war

CAPTAIN an army officer ranking next above **lieutenant**

CENSOR the removal of information thought to be harmful to a country's security

We'll have to change that – it will damage morale.

CIVILIAN people who are not members of the police force or the army

COLONEL an army officer in command of a regiment, immediately below a brigadier in rank

COMPANY a unit of soldiers normally made up of 100 men

CONSCRIPTION a law requiring all men of a certain age to join the armed forces and be available if called to fight at any time

READ ALL ABOUT IT

CONSCRIPTION INTRODUCED BY GOVERNMENT

CONTEXT the circumstances and background to a situation

CORPORAL an army officer ranking below a **sergeant**

CRUMPS a slang word for a heavy shell explosion

CURTAIN FIRE a heavy shower of bullets

DUGOUTS a hollowed-out roofed shelter

FORCED LABOUR compulsory, unpaid work

GURKHAS soldiers from Nepal serving in the British army

HUN a slang word for a German person

HOWITZER a large gun that fires very big shells high into the air

INFERENCE the gaining of information indirectly from surrounding evidence

JUNIOR OFFICER a low ranking officer

LIEUTENANT an officer serving just below the **captain**

LIMBER a two-wheeled vehicle with a gun attached to it

NO MAN'S LAND the narrow stretch of land separating the German and **Allied** trenches

PROVENANCE origin or starting point

REGIMENT a unit of the army commanded by a colonel and made up of several **companies**

SECOND LIEUTENANT an officer serving directly below a **lieutenant**

SERGEANT a soldier ranking above **corporal**

SOSs a slang term meaning rescue missions

TOMMY a slang word for a British soldier

MORTAR a large portable gun that fires shells over short distances

MUTINY a situation where soldiers refuse to obey orders and violently attempt to take control away from their leaders

ORIENTATE to familiarise yourself with a situation

PLATOON a unit of soldiers normally made up of 50 men

PRIVATE a soldier of the lowest rank in the army

PROPAGANDA ideas and facts deliberately spread to influence people's opinions

WESTERN FRONT the area of military operations running from Belgium, through Northern France to the Swiss border

◆ Index

THIS IS HISTORY!

◆ Titles in the series

Pupils' Books (PB) and Teachers' Resource Books (TRB) are available for all titles.

Write Your Own Roman Story	**PB** 0 7195 7717 9	**TRB** 0 7195 7718 7
The Norman Conquest	**PB** 0 7195 8555 4	**TRB** 0 7195 8556 2
King John	**PB** 0 7195 8539 2	**TRB** 0 7195 8540 6
Lost in Time	**PB** 0 7195 8557 0	**TRB** 0 7195 8558 9
'King' Cromwell?	**PB** 0 7195 8559 7	**TRB** 0 7195 8560 0
The Impact of Empire	**PB** 0 7195 8561 9	**TRB** 0 7195 8562 7
Dying for the Vote!	**PB** 0 7195 8563 5	**TRB** 0 7195 8564 3
The Trenches	**PB** 0 7195 8565 1	**TRB** 0 7195 8566 X
The Holocaust	**PB** 0 7195 7709 8	**TRB** 0 7195 7710 1
The Twentieth Century	**PB** 0 7195 7711 X	**TRB** 0 7195 7712 8

◆ Acknowledgements

Pictures:
pp.4, **6**, **8-10** *all*, **14-16**, **24** *all*, **25** *t*, *c* and *bl* Imperial War Museum, London; **p.25** *br* Hulton Getty; **p.26** Topham Picturepoint; **pp.27** *t* and *b*, **36** and **37** Imperial War Museum, London; **pp.38** and **39** *all* The Illustrated London News Picture Library; **p.40** National Portrait Gallery, London; **pp.41** and **42** Hulton Getty; **pp.52** and **55** *tl* The Illustrated London News Picture Library; **p.55** *tr* Imperial War Museum, London; **p.56** Jacket cover from *Birdsong* by Sebastian Faulks published by Hutchinson. Used by permission of The Random House Group Limited; **pp.58** and **59** BBC Library.

(*t* – top, *b* = bottom, *r* = right, *l* = left, *c* = centre)

Written sources:
p. 16 (Source 3) from Roger Smither et al, *Viewing Guide to 'The Battle of the Somme' film* (Film Archive, Imperial War Museum, 1987); **p. 27** (Source 12) from Lyn Macdonald, *1914–1918: Voices and Images of the Great War* (Michael Joseph, 1991), © Lyn Macdonald, 1988. Reproduced by permission of Penguin Books Ltd; **p.28** (Source 13) from Lyn Macdonald, *1914–1918: Voices and Images of the Great War* (Michael Joseph, 1991), © Lyn Macdonald, 1988. Reproduced by permission of Penguin Books Ltd; (Source 14) from the Department of Documents, Imperial War Museum. Reproduced by permission of Mr S D Chater; (Source 15) from Lyn Macdonald, *1914–1918: Voices and Images of the Great War* (Michael Joseph, 1991), © Lyn Macdonald, 1988. Reproduced by permission of Penguin Books Ltd; **p. 30** (Source 18) from Robert Graves, *Goodbye To All That*, (Carcanet Press, 1929); (Source 20) from George Coppard, *With a Machine-Gun to Cambrai*, © with permission of the Controller of Her Majesty's Stationery Office; **p. 31** (Source 21) from Lyn Macdonald, *1914–1918: Voices and Images of the Great War*

(Michael Joseph, 1991), © Lyn Macdonald, 1988. Reproduced by permission of Penguin Books Ltd; **p. 32** (Sources 22 and 23) from Lyn Macdonald, *1914–1918: Voices and Images of the Great War* (Michael Joseph, 1991), © Lyn Macdonald, 1988. Reproduced by permission of Penguin Books Ltd; **p. 33** (Source 24) from Lyn Macdonald, *1914–1918: Voices and Images of the Great War* (Michael Joseph, 1991), © Lyn Macdonald, 1988. Reproduced by permission of Penguin Books Ltd; (Sources 25 and 26) from Lyn Macdonald, *1914–1918: Voices and Images of the Great War* (Michael Joseph, 1991), © Lyn Macdonald, 1988. Reproduced by permission of Penguin Books Ltd; **p.40** (Source 35) 'Dulce et Decorum Est' by Wilfred Owen; **p. 41** (Sources 36–38) Copyright Siegfried Sassoon by kind permission of George Sassoon; **p. 42** (Source 39) taken from Robert Giddings, *The War Poets* (Bloomsbury, 1988); (Source 40) © The estate of Richard Aldington; (Source 41) from Lyn Macdonald, *1914–1918: Voices and Images of the Great War* (Michael Joseph, 1991), © Lyn Macdonald, 1988. Reproduced by permission of Penguin Books Ltd; **p. 54** (Sources 3 and 7) from Lyn Macdonald, *1914–1918: Voices and Images of the Great War* (Michael Joseph, 1991), © Lyn Macdonald, 1988. Reproduced by permission of Penguin Books Ltd; (Source 5) from Niall Ferguson (Allen Lane, The Penguin Press, 1998) © Niall Ferguson, 1998; **p. 55** (Source 13) from Robert Graves, *Complete Poems* (Carcanet Press, 2000); **p. 56** (Source 1) from *Birdsong* by Sebastian Faulks, published by Hutchinson/Vintage. Reprinted by permission of The Random House Group Ltd; **p. 58** (Source 2) extracts *from Blackadder: The Whole Damn Dynasty* (Michael Joseph, 1988), © Richard Curtis and Ben Elton, 1987.

While every effort has been made to contact copyright holders, the publishers apologise for any omissions, which they will be pleased to rectify at the earliest opportunity.